"Jim Putman is a coach at heart. He is a leader of people, and they follow him. He is committed, authentic, and refreshingly honest. What you see is what you get. . . . He boils everything down to its essence and is not distracted. But at the core he cares. He cares for people and believes that one sheep should not be lost no matter what it costs the shepherd. You cannot read this book with an open heart and remain nonchalant about the people God has put in your care."

—From the foreword by **Avery Willis**,
author and international speaker

"Time out . . . this one's the real deal! Jim Putman does an awesome job of challenging Christian leaders to rethink the boxes we find ourselves in. *Church Is a Team Sport* is a gutsy book that promotes innovative and practical means for how to become a true team. There's no trash talking here, just positive lessons to improve your church."

—**Dave Stone**, senior pastor,
Southeast Christian Church, Louisville, Kentucky

"Jim Putman's compelling new book grabbed me from page one. I read it in one sitting and predict you will too. This is the ultimate textbook (after the Bible) for growing churches and making disciples. It's a championship strategy all the way."

—**Pat Williams**, senior vice president, Orlando Magic;
author, *Read for Your Life*

"Jim Putman has written a clear, practical, and powerful guide for doing church together, as a team. His authenticity is refreshing and the story of Real Life is amazing. Pick up a copy of this book for yourself and for your team."

—**Jud Wilhite**, author, *Stripped*; senior pastor,
Central Christian Church, Las Vegas

"Jim's story of going from frustration with Christians to loving Jesus and leading people to serve the local community resonated deep within my heart. Any man who likes athletics and is tired of the typical churchy jargon should read this book. It's a winner!"

—**Paul Byrd**, Cleveland
Indians pitcher

"After forty years as a senior minister and five decades as a determined, but amateur athlete, I have often marveled at the similarities between pastoring a church and competing in sports. Both require, among other things, dedication, hard work, and discipline. Now, Jim Putman has written a practical and thoroughly readable book that makes that comparison between sports and church. In the process, he reveals the principles that can help your church grow, win souls to Christ, and make disciples. After reading Jim's book, you'll understand why the church he started has been called 'the fastest growing nondenominational Christian church in America.'"

—**Bob Russell**, author; speaker; and former pastor,
Southeast Christian Church, Louisville, Kentucky

"Fantastic read!!! We all play a role. Putman challenges the star and the benchwarmer alike to understand this: Each one of us is called to unity in one goal and purpose—playing and winning for the Ultimate Coach."

—**Will Dawson**, sports reporter/producer,
Christian Broadcasting Network

"Growing a church from a handful of people to a morning worship attendance that has already exceeded the 8,000 mark, in less than ten years, is a remarkable achievement. Having the majority of those involved in a small group, ministering to one another, is nothing short of miraculous.

"Jim Putman gives us a peek inside the playbook that has been used to build one of America's largest and strongest churches. These are not the untested theories of some ivory tower theologian. I've had the privilege of preaching at Jim's church and have seen these principles at work in the lives of his people.

"This is a book for winners. A book for pastors and people (coaches and players) who want to build a championship-caliber church that, year after year, will honor God, reach the lost, equip the saints, impact society, and result in changed lives for eternity. God always meant for His church to win. In this new book, Jim Putman shows us how."

—**Barry L. Cameron**, senior pastor, Crossroads Christian Church, Grand Prairie, Texas; author, *The ABC's of Financial Success* and *Contagious Generosity*

"Caution! Don't read this book unless you want a biblical vision and strategy of how to turn the average anemic church into a winner. Written in an engaging and understandable way, Pastor Jim Putman transports our minds from mediocre Christianity and boring church experiences to the excitement of winning—being all that Jesus Christ intended. This book is a must for every Christian and church leader."

—Dr. **Richard A. Rollins**, executive pastor, Valley Bible Church, Hercules, California; coauthor, *Redeeming Relationships*

"*Church Is a Team Sport* is written by one of America's great pastors, or should I say 'coaches' for successful living. Jim Putman outlines a clear path for a healthy church, both emphasizing and explaining the vital role of key players on a winning team. This book should be read by anyone and everyone involved in church work, and by anyone helping others live like champions."

—**Tommy Barnett**, pastor, Phoenix First Assembly; co-pastor, Los Angeles Dream Center

"Although I have worked with the concept of sports and Christians for a long time, I've never been comfortable with direct faith-to-sports analogies such as 'God as the head coach' and 'the Bible as the playbook.' These often seem to demean rather than lift up our heavenly Father or even our faith. However, in *Church Is a Team Sport*, Jim Putman has successfully used the metaphor of the church as a team sport. Through citing his own negative experiences in the local church and contrasting it with a hopeful new way of looking at the church—all while maintaining a well-crafted sports analogy—Putman elevates faith elements that should be treated with utmost respect. Putman's presentation of a church concept based on relational living and strong biblical teaching is a valuable tool for leaders of churches of any size who want to minister to real people with Christ's love and godly principles."

—**Dave Branon**, managing editor, *Sports Spectrum* magazine; writer, *Our Daily Bread*

"I have observed Jim and his ministry up close for several years. He is a great coach, pastor, and leader. This book is not theory. It is a practical playbook that has been used at Real Life to develop a winning church. Jim's insights will help your church become more effective in impacting your community. All of your leadership team needs to read this book."

—**Don Wilson**, pastor, Christ's Church of the Valley, Phoenix, Arizona

"This book is not just readable, it is compelling and authentic! I have personally experienced the ministry of Jim Putman, his team, and Real Life Ministries since they were just three months old. The growth has been nothing short of miraculous. Many times they faced specific hurdles, but through perseverance they have continued on a phenomenal growth pattern. We have all seen the development and expansion of their ministry, but more important than the numbers are the touching of lives and successful evangelistic program to expand the Kingdom. This has really been amazing to watch! I firmly believe under Jim's leadership Real Life Ministries has followed Acts 2:42 and has carried out the Great Commission of Matthew 28. The personalization and principles in this book are a practical reality for others and can help expand the church in today's chaotic world. Jim's passion for ministry and reaching the lost are reflected throughout each word, each paragraph, and each chapter!"

—**Douglas J. Crozier**, president, Church Development Fund, Inc.

Drawing from his years as both athlete and coach, Jim Putman gives us fresh insight into the team dynamics of the local church. Whether a rookie in the Christian life or seasoned minister, you'll come away from this book with a new appreciation of what makes a local church a team of champions.

—**David Stevens**, senior pastor, Central Bible Church, Portland, Oregon

Church
Is a
Team Sport

**A Championship
Strategy for
Doing Ministry Together**

Jim Putman

BakerBooks
Grand Rapids, Michigan

© 2008 by Jim Putman

Published by Baker Books
a division of Baker Publishing Group
P.O. Box 6287, Grand Rapids, MI 49516-6287
www.bakerbooks.com

Printed in the United States of America

Library of Congress Cataloging-in-Publication Data
Putman, Jim, 1966–
    Church is a team sport : a championship strategy for doing ministry together / Jim Putman.
        p.   cm.
    Includes bibliographical references.
    ISBN 978-0-8010-1302-7 (cloth)
    ISBN 978-0-8010-7162-1 (ITPE)
    1. Church growth. I. Title.
BV652.25.P78 2008
253—dc22   2007034119

Published in association with the literary agency of Sanford Communications, Inc., 16778 S.E. Cohiba Ct., Damascus, OR 97089.

To my Lord and Savior Jesus Christ who saved me though I was a sinful man. I find it amazing that He not only saved me but allowed me to be a part of His team. To my wife, Lori, who has helped shape me over the years. She put up with the man I was and was patient as the Lord did His work and continues to do it. She has gone along for the ride that has been ministry. To my sons Christian, Jesse, and Will, who have been my greatest joy. I love them more than life. To my father and mother, Bill and Bobbi Putman, who never gave up on me when I rejected Jesus and them. For all the nights I awoke to them praying for me. They were the prodigal son's father waiting for their child to come home.

To Aaron and Kelly Couch and family—I have your back no matter where you go.

To Jim and Cassi Harris—who gave up so much to be a part of this adventure.

To Larry and Judy Bennet—who kept me in ministry when I was almost done.

To David Elmes, Christina Detwiler, Bill Buley, and Lydia Grubb— thank you for your help. Without you this would have never been finished.

To the Backyard Gang—I love you all.

To the elders at Real Life—you are truly God's men.

To the executive team—Brandon Guindon, Lance Wigton, Craig Miles, Bill Krause, Bill Lehman, Toodie Ward—my true friends and partners.

To the staff at Real Life—I would go to battle alongside of you anytime, anywhere.

To the Real Life Ministries family—I am so proud of all who serve in our church—you are truly a people on a mission. I have never seen people who try harder.

To Doug Crozier and CDF—thanks for the friendship and partnership.

To the team at Sanford Communications—thanks for your literary and editorial assistance with this book.

And to the team at Baker Publishing Group—thanks for your enthusiastic and skillful support.

CONTENTS

9

Contents

FOREWORD

by Avery Willis

Would you like to see what a first-century church would look like in the twenty-first century? Check out Real Life Ministries Church. Of course, there are obvious differences, but the key is in the similarities on the most fundamental levels.

The story of Real Life grows out of the story of Jim Putman. Jim was a national championship wrestler and then a coach of championship wrestlers before he lost his wrestling match with God. In *Church Is a Team Sport*, Jim uses the analogy of coaching and teamwork to show how God built Real Life's team from two couples to over eight thousand people in eight years—all in a northern Idaho town of ten thousand people. Jim never intended to start a megachurch. He is as surprised at the thousands of new believers as Peter must have been at Pentecost.

As Jim contemplated a church plant, he was dismayed at the majority of churches in America that are not growing. And he was tired of twentieth-century church accretions and infighting. Jim pulls no punches. Like any good coach, he tells things as they are.

When he started Real Life, he wanted to get back to the primary task of the church—making disciples. Many churches assume they can make disciples incidentally, but Real Life makes disciples intentionally. Jim does not try to be the star of a show. He makes disciples and equips leaders to live as disciples of Christ.

I have had the opportunity to look inside this church as a consultant for more than a year, and I am often asked, "Is this the real deal?" Yes, this is the real deal. Read the book and judge for yourself. Real Life's vision is to fulfill the Great Commission. Following are some of the unique ways they are accomplishing this vision.

Disciple Making. Their vision to make disciples is the determining factor in everything they do. Most churches make it one of many emphases, hoping disciple making will take place by osmosis. At Real Life, however, if an activity does not contribute to making disciples, it takes a backseat. This church uses a clear, simple process: Share, Connect, Minister, and Disciple. Making disciples is helping people follow Jesus in all areas of life.

A Relational Context. Real Life makes disciples *in a relational context.* That means making disciples in small groups. They believe that you can't make disciples in a vacuum such as a class where you just pass on information. In their six hundred small groups, they deal with real life and follow it up by working on discipleship in everyday relationships. In every large worship service, the leaders emphasize that people must get connected to a small group in order to grow.

Unity. Disunity in the church drove Jim Putman from the church and the faith of his father. When God led him to start a church, he resolved that unity would be a core value. Real Life focuses on the basic doctrines of the Bible but will not get sidetracked with peripheral issues. There is agreement on essentials, but the people of Real Life are respectful of others' opinions on nonessentials. If you want to debate a doctrine that is not essential to salvation, they won't go there. They value unity more than unanimity in the details. New members commit themselves to biblical beliefs embraced by the church and commit to avoid arguing over nonessential Christian doctrines.

Ministry. Ministry takes place in small groups, but it does not stop there. The church meets the needs of hundreds of needy people every month. People come to the church to get help, and Real Life meets them right where they are. For example, more than six hundred people are in recovery groups every week.

Evangelism. Evangelism is a natural outgrowth of all the things mentioned above. Because people get help in their small group, they naturally tell their friends. Every event sponsored by the church has the purpose of introducing people to Christ and making disciples. When people come to Christ, they are baptized by the small group or those who helped them to faith in Christ. As they practice Acts 2:42–47, the Lord adds to their number daily those who are being saved.

Leadership Development. Because the goal is making disciples, Real Life is always looking for new leaders. The church trains them in the essentials of disciple making and shepherding, and then holds them accountable to the team and to the Lord. Every disciple is a leader in the making.

Teamwork. The name of the book hints that a winning team is the defining work of a coach. At Real Life they have one goal—winning. Winning is defined as making disciples who are like Christ. Every player is important. Theirs is a culture of excellence and hard work that focuses on results instead of a show.

Innovation. For Real Life innovation is not doing something that no other church has done. It is getting back to the basics and living as disciples. I have been surprised at their willingness to change. After I shared with Jim that according to the Department of Education over half the people in the United States are oral learners, he asked me to teach the staff and small group leaders how to tell and use Bible stories to shape the worldview of the people. As this book goes to press, their small groups are using a set of Bible stories to paint a panorama from creation to Christ on the hearts of the people. I was amazed with their response after they had been so successful with what they were doing. They will do whatever it takes to grow disciples.

❖

Jim Putman is a coach at heart. He is a leader of people, and they follow him. He is committed, authentic, and refreshingly honest. What you see is what you get. He is strong in his convictions. He keeps to the basics and is unrelenting on essentials. He is focused. He boils everything down to its essence and is not distracted. But at the core he cares. He cares for people and believes that one sheep should not be lost no matter what it costs the shepherd. You cannot read this book with an open heart and remain nonchalant about the people God has put in your care.

PREFACE

This book is written for all of those who acknowledge that something is wrong with the box they were handed. By the box, I mean the church. Something is wrong and they know it. Maybe they cannot put their finger on what it is, but they see what the church was supposed to be and what it is, and they are discouraged. Many wrongly believe they can be all right with God but not be involved with the body of Christ. I do not believe this is biblical, or healthy. I believe there are some real answers to the problems the church currently faces. They are not easy—greatness never is—but we really do have the ability to change things.

I believe that all Christians are a part of the Royal Priesthood, the Holy nation, so this book is written to all who would read it. You will notice this book is predominantly directed to male leadership. I do believe the principles will work in any team situation (women, children, etc.). My hope is that those in church leadership will decide to test what is written in this book with the Word of God, and seek to make changes as they are led by the Holy Spirit.

My training in leadership comes from athletics and coaching; therefore, many of the metaphors used in this book are from that background. It fits in my mind, because I see the church as the Lord's team. The opponent of the church is the devil. The playing field is the earth. The players are the people. The leaders are the coaches. As I read the Scriptures, I see team everywhere. Teams have a common purpose; they run the same play at the same time and work together in their respective positions. I also believe that most Americans understand sports far better than they do the church. So I've used language that is familiar to most of us in order to explain what I see going on in the church.

I understand that no writer connects with everyone. For those of you who are not sports enthusiasts, my hope is that you will understand the concepts and be able to transfer them into your own language with your teams in a useful way. For example, if you are a musician, you might use a band analogy. Band teachers know that they must get everyone to understand their part using the same sheet of music. In any case, my hope is that these biblical concepts can be used to make the church a force to be reckoned with again.

Acknowledgments

Eight years ago, this grand adventure called Real Life Ministries began. I feel as if it has been twenty-five years. The people who started with us have become my best friends and family. They have been a part of shaping me and my family as well as my ministry beliefs. We have truly been a team.

As a team we were led by God to design what we have now. As a team we will go into the future. My whole ministry career I wanted to be as the Scripture described Paul and Barnabas, or Luke and Timothy; as they did, I wanted to walk with my friends into the fight. I wanted to have accountability, and to have friends who were not in ministry for the money or position. I wanted to walk with fellow warriors who were willing to risk all for the right fight. I wanted to be able to know that my friends would be loyal enough to fight beside me and faithful enough to fight me if I needed it.

I wanted to be a part of a miracle instead of just hearing about one. It has not been easy, but it has been worth it. Most of what I know came from my parents setting me on their shoulders, so to speak, and allowing me to start from a higher place than they did. My father has helped me to see farther because of how he allowed God to direct his life.

God has brought friends at the right time—Aaron, Brandon, Lance, Bill, and many others who have played a huge part in my

17

personal life. The staff, elders, and other leaders, though we have disagreed at times, we have still moved forward. We have been able to see the differences as blessings in disguise. I do not believe anyone sees the whole picture in ministry—that is why we need each other.

God has brought great men into my life at the right time to help me when I have been at a loss as to what to do next. God has brought people from our church into the life of our family when we needed it. Some saw we were tired and sent us away for much-needed rest. Some (Dan Lynch, Charlie Couch, Doug Smoot) gave me great advice about being a husband and father. Doug Crozier has been a great friend. Avery Willis came into the life of our church at just the right time; he has led us into some new paths that I think will take us to the next stage of our development.

As I look back, I see God has done so much and I am excited to see what will come next. I no longer have an unrealistic view of what it takes to go forward. It has cost us much as a church and as a family, but I believe it is worth it. I have much to learn, and my team and I must cross many more crossroads. However, I know that I will face the giants in the land with a group of believers who will fight. I will face them with a group of friends who are as loyal as you can get. I will face them with a wife who will love me no matter what. I will have the greatest thing of all as well. I have a God who uses simple people. I have a God who keeps His promises and who will bring the answers at the right time if we seek Him together. Ultimately, He cares more about His mission than I do. I pray that we continue to decrease so that Jesus may increase.

INTRODUCTION

The Real Life Story

The year 1997 was a major turning point in my life. After serving as a youth minister for ten years in two churches where the youth ministry grew but the adult church did not, God made it clear: *It's time to help the kids by doing something about the adults.* I certainly hadn't stopped caring about kids, but it was so disheartening to watch these kids we had won and raised in the Lord have nowhere to go as they became adults.

In my heart I believed the Lord could use the ministry philosophies we had developed for the youth to create positive, healthy, dynamic changes within the church as a whole. The only question for me to answer was "Where?"

Still, I was shocked when God's next call for me came through the phone.

THE CALL

One day, God prompted Jim and Lydia Grubb, a couple I had never met, to call me on the phone. They told me God had given them a burning desire to plant a new church in northern Idaho. Along with another couple, Jeff and Debbie Ross, they had been

19

praying for about a year for a nondenominational church to be started in their area. There wasn't much money for a church plant—they had talked to one small church that might be able to help. I then asked how they had obtained my name. They originally contacted my father, who had been in charge of three church-planting organizations. He told them I would do a great job, but he doubted I would be interested because I was experiencing success in youth ministry at a church in Oregon City, Oregon.

I had no desire to plant a church, even though I grew up in a church planter's home. As a child, I moved every two years because my father would begin a new work in an area that previously didn't have a nondenominational church. Each church started with seven people—my dad, my mom, and the five of us kids. We were the ones who put up chairs, took them down, put up walls for classrooms, laid down carpet, and brought in hymnals, communion stuff, a pulpit, a piano, and overhead projectors every week. I lost countless hours of sleep due to these early morning setup sessions, and missed many an NFL football game on Sunday afternoons.

I hated the idea of church planting. The instant they asked me if I had an interest in planting this new church, those memories flooded my mind, and I rationalized there was no way this was from God. Even if I were to plant a church, I would never do it alone. My father had always started churches alone—he was the youth pastor, the counselor, the worship leader, the setup crew, and usually his own secretary. I never saw my dad! My mother was involved in everything too. I have three boys, and there is no way the Lord would want me to go into a situation like that by myself! There was no money for even one church planter, let alone a team.

No way would I even consider it.

Jim and Lydia asked me to pray about it. I assured them I would. Actually, I had no intention of praying about it. I told myself there was no way this was God's idea. Later, I mentioned the phone call to Aaron Couch, the young adult pastor at the church I was working in at the time. I knew he would agree it was crazy—not from God. But he didn't. He immediately prodded, "Why not?"

I quickly evaded the question. I didn't want to hear it. I didn't want to discuss it. The whole idea annoyed me. Not long after the first phone call from Coeur d'Alene, Idaho, I got another call from Jim, Lydia, Jeff, and Debbie.

Man, they're persistent, I thought.

When I had talked with them in November, I had let it slip that I would be bringing the Oregon City high school wrestling team I was coaching to a tournament at North Idaho College just before Christmas. They wanted to meet with me. I reluctantly agreed. Then I asked Aaron to drive up with me to meet with them, because I knew he wouldn't leave me alone in this situation, and once he met these crazy people he would back off and recognize it couldn't be from God.

After getting my team off to bed for the night, we met with the two couples in our hotel room. I must admit it was a meeting for the ages. These people were not crazy at all. They were godly people who really felt God wanted to do something special in that little area in northern Idaho.

At the end of the meeting, they asked me to pray about it. This time when I agreed, I meant it. Aaron was excited and wanted to be in on the praying process too.

I remember thinking, *Lord, if you want me to come to this place, you will have to change my heart*. I also told God, even if He did change my heart, He would have to do a miracle. There was no way the money was there to plant a church.

God Works in Mysterious Ways

A week and a half later, I was at another tournament, and God performed a miracle I will never forget! At this point, I had decided it was time to leave Oregon City. I hadn't really decided where the Lord was leading, but I knew God would give direction.

One of my main concerns about leaving was finding a good coach for the kids on my team. I had a deep love for them. Many had given their lives to Christ and were coming to youth group. All of my coaching staff had become Christians, and I wanted to bring in a coach who cared about more than just wrestling. My preference was a Christian coach, but I did not know any who would be willing to come. At the least, I wanted a moral man who cared about kids. During a break in the wrestling tournament, I walked up to Coach Roy, a man who coached in an area high school. I knew Roy cared about his kids, and they loved him too. I never heard him swear, and he treated his kids with respect. "Roy," I said, "I am going to be leaving, and I wonder if you would consider applying for my job at Oregon City?"

"What do you mean, you're leaving?" he asked. "This team is good and is getting better every year!"

Roy was right—we finally had a successful little kids' program, and were reaping the benefits. We had several national champions in the junior high, and things were really looking up. I explained to him how coaching was just an opportunity for me to get on the campus of the schools. My real goal was to get into the lives of the kids in the area and guide them to our church's youth ministry. He asked, "Where do you plan to go?"

I told him I didn't know, but I was going on to be an adult pastor. He asked me where I'd like to go if I could go anywhere. I shocked even myself when I responded, "Northern Idaho." Even as I said it, I could not believe my own words. Where did that come from? How had I come to this place where I would choose a church plant?

Roy asked, "What's keeping you from going there?" I told him if I were to go, I would go with a team, and that takes money. I explained that usually there were church-planting organizations that funded church startups. Sometimes a church would plant another church, but most barely had enough to fund their own ministries. He asked how much it would cost to plant a church. Truthfully, I hadn't really considered that. It took me a couple of seconds to think about what would be involved with such a venture: equipment, salaries, fliers, a place to meet, children's ministry supplies—there was a lot to consider.

I threw out a number: "Thirty thousand dollars." (I didn't know that church plants usually started with hundreds of thousands.)

Roy just looked at me for a few seconds and then responded: "I'll give you thirty thousand dollars." I laughed. I thought he was kidding.

I joked, "What do they pay you schoolteachers around here?" After he chuckled, he told me that he wasn't a teacher either; he too coached on the side. He went on to tell me of the multiple big businesses he owned and that he had made millions just the month before.

My jaw dropped.

"Jim," he said, "I have a deal that has been held up for the last year. If you will pray that it goes through, and it does, I will give you the thirty thousand dollars to start that church!"

After trying to digest his words, I quietly spoke. "Roy, I didn't know that you were a Christian."

He said, "Oh, I'm not sure what I am. One day my Learjet broke down, and I had to ride first class on a commercial plane. When I sat down, there was a book sitting in my seat. I didn't have anything else to read, so I picked it up. It was called *Left Behind*. Have you ever heard of it? That book scared the hell out of me!"

I got the chance to answer some of his questions, and Roy told me that he had been contemplating giving his life to Christ and that this conversation must be a God thing.

That night when I got home I told my wife, Lori, the amazing story. Then I called my new friends in northern Idaho. I told them to start praying, and I began to pray like I had never prayed before. I felt as if the Lord was telling me to trust Him like I had never trusted before. God always worked in my life when I would let Him, but something strange was starting to happen—I felt like I was on a ride I had never been on before.

I called Roy and told him I had asked our group to pray. Then I ventured, "Roy, you shared with me how much you made last month, so I want to say, if you have thirty thousand dollars, then you have fifty thousand dollars. I want you to consider giving more."

Roy laughed and told me I was right. "You keep praying that this deal goes through, and I *will* give you fifty thousand dollars."

Well, that was enough for me. God had made it clear. In the next few months, I told my church in Oregon City I would be leaving in six months. Aaron let them know that he was going with me. We drove to Coeur d'Alene to meet the families and begin searching for other churches that might want to help. We called Roy from time to time to see if the deal had gone through. Each time he told me no, but urged me to keep praying.

Two things happened during this time that prodded us to step out further in faith. A little church in central Idaho called to tell us they believed God wanted them to help. Grangeville Christian Church agreed to send $250 a month to support our work. The amount was small compared to the need, but to us it was confirmation that God was going to come through with the money from Roy.

Then, a church-planting association from southern Idaho called us to say they would give us $1,000 a month for two years. The next day we received another call; this one came from First Christian Church in Sandpoint. They were located forty-five miles north of Post Falls, the town where we would plant the church. They agreed to give $1,000 a month. Though this didn't come close to the need, it was further confirmation that God was working.

MUSIC TO OUR EARS

As all church planters know, music plays a huge part in a Sunday morning service. We had some in our new group who had musical abilities, but no one to take charge and make it happen, until one day I got another phone call.

My brother-in-law, Jim Harris, had been attending Cincinnati Bible College and called to let me know he was getting married to Cassi, a beautiful Christian young lady. He also shared he had some ministry opportunities to consider as graduation was approaching. After he filled Lori and me in on the details, I shared with him what we were intending to do.

He listened intently, spoke more about his upcoming marriage, and then said goodbye. A few days later, Jim called back. I will never forget the conversation. He told me that he and Cassi had been praying and talking, and they had decided to come to Idaho to help us.

My first thought was that he had misunderstood me. Had I somehow given him the idea that I was offering him a job? I tried to explain that we had no money to hire anyone. He said, "We're not coming for money. We believe God wants us to come help you plant the church, and we intend to get jobs to pay our own way."

I couldn't believe it. Here they were, graduating with degrees and being offered paying jobs, but they were coming to help us for free. It didn't make sense, but it was great! Jim was going to lead music and Cassi was going to help with children's ministry.

The day we got Jim's call, we checked in again with Roy. There was no news yet, but we kept praying. We knew God was laying out seeds of encouragement. We knew he was going to make it happen. We decided we would leave Oregon City at the end of May. I started flying to northern Idaho on Sunday nights to do a Bible study and returned each Monday morning to Oregon. During that time, our little group grew from four to fifteen.

We began looking for houses in Coeur d'Alene. People around us thought we were crazy. After all, even if the money came in from Roy, including all the other expenses, it would only pay our salaries for three months. We stood firm, believing God had told us to go and we were going!

People asked, "Aren't you nervous you have already told your church you are resigning but the money hasn't come in yet?" I must admit, as the months went by, we were getting nervous. But we decided to believe, rather than doubt. After all, look at what God had done so far.

Three weeks before moving day, Roy called. "I don't know how it happened, but the deal just went through. Come and pick up your check!"

THE BEGINNING

The first part of June 1998, Aaron Couch, his wife Kelli, Lori, and I packed up the kids and all our things and headed for Post Falls, Idaho. We moved into our homes and we hit the ground running. We started meeting with everybody who was interested in the new plant. We met with those who had been fervently praying. The Lord started to bring people to us.

We were excited about what the Lord was doing in our lives, and we were fearless enough to tell anyone who would listen. We told them what God had already done and what He had put on our hearts to do. Most people thought we were crazy, but a few here and there drifted in to check out our little group.

I remember the day we went to buy a computer. The salesman asked why we needed it, so we told him we had just started a new church. He asked how many of us there were, so we told him: "Twenty, at this point."

He asked if I was a pastor. I told him that I was a youth minister learning how to be a pastor. He asked me to pray for him. He told me his wife had left him for his best friend and that he had lost everything. He was working in this computer shop just to make enough to keep his house (which he later lost). We did pray with him and invited him to our backyard Bible study. In September, we baptized him in the lake in the middle of town. Our first conversion had taken place!

After about two months, our group had grown to about thirty-five people, including fifteen kids. We needed something bigger to meet in as we were now filling the backyard with adults and the front yard with kids. Office space was very expensive, and we wanted to be good stewards. God opened the door to an old broken-down house with a shop. We cleaned up the house and used it for children's classrooms and began to remodel the shop. People helped as they could after work and on weekends, but the bulk of the work fell on Aaron and me. We almost killed each other trying to take out walls, lay carpet, and get it ready for offices and our first meeting room. We had grown to fifty people in two and a half months and desperately needed a place to meet. I have never been able to work well with my hands. If I couldn't get it done on an athletic field or with my mouth, it usually didn't get done well. During those days, I learned a lot about myself and about the team God was bringing together. Those times allowed everyone to pitch in, and it went a long way toward building a team.

After weeks of working on our shack, we were finally able to have our first study in August. It had no insulation, air-conditioning, or heat, and the bathroom worked only occasionally. Not long after we moved in, we knew we had to start looking for a place to hold services. The shop could hold only so many for a Bible study, and there was no way to have a worship service where we could invite others to join us.

The first place we went was the local school system. They informed us that they would not allow any church group to meet in their facilities for longer than six months. We could not start a church in something so temporary, so we started looking for an empty building or storefront. We were blown away by how much they wanted for rent. We contemplated moving to a nearby city that had cheaper buildings, but we felt that God wanted us in Post Falls. We were getting discouraged, but we just kept praying. One day, as I was driving on the freeway to Spokane, I noticed a new theatre off to the right. I thought to myself, *I wonder if they would be interested in letting us meet there?*

I pulled off the freeway into the parking lot. The place was dark, but there was one car in front of the building. I almost drove away; it was in the middle of the day and they did not have a movie showing until that evening. I decided to check the door, and to my surprise, it opened.

When I walked in, there was a lady in the lobby crying. I approached her, completely forgetting why I had come. In the next hour I had the opportunity to share my faith with this lady who was having marital problems. By the end of our conversation, she was ready to accept Christ. After praying together, she said, "Enough about me. Why did you come in here?" I shared with her our dilemma. She recommended I talk to the owner. She said he was hurting financially and just might allow us to use the building on Sunday mornings. I asked if he was a Christian. She said that she didn't know but that he had gone to Promise Keepers once.

That night I called him, and after a short conversation he agreed to let us use the theater. At first he came to our services to make sure we were not tearing up the building or getting into the concessions. Not long afterward, he and his wife started attending. Later his seventy-year-old, non-Christian father started coming. Then the owner's son and daughter-in-law started coming. Eventually his ninety-two-year-old grandmother came—and all of them gave their lives to the Lord. In fact, Brandon Guindon, the theatre owner's son, is now the team leader over all small groups. God has used him to help grow our small groups from five to more than seven hundred groups in eight years.

RAMPING UP

Now that we had a place to hold worship services, we had to get ready for our launch. God continued to work in amazing ways. It wasn't long after we received permission to move into the theatre that a small church shut its doors and gave us all they had. It included a very old sound system and some children's materials that were probably twenty-five years old, but it was an answer to prayer. Another church gave us an overhead projector for our worship lyrics, and fifty folding chairs. One of our families, Dave and Laura Wismer, who had recently moved to the area following God's promptings, spent days building our children's ministry tables and benches. They were perfect, not because they were beautiful, but because they were made with love. We were all set to have Sunday morning services.

We had another problem—or so we thought. Advertising can be very expensive. We had made some fliers and our handful of families handed them out, but we wanted to reach the entire area to let people know we were starting. God provided again. Bill, a reporter for the local paper, asked if he could do a story on our new church plant. He thought we were crazy for coming to northern Idaho with three months' salary, buying houses, and starting with four families. The circulation for the paper was about 25,000. The article ran on the front page and coincided with our start-up date. God had provided our advertising for free.

While all of the details for starting a Sunday morning service were being worked out, we continued to meet in small groups. We trained people who had never been involved in church before. We did many things together, becoming a family. When someone was missing, we called to make sure they were okay. When someone was in the hospital, we visited. When someone was sick, we made meals. We celebrated together whenever there was something to celebrate.

AN OFFICIAL BEGINNING

On October 18, 1998, we had our official first service. It was a glorious day—and everything that could go wrong did. We had a single guitar, a bad sound system, ministry equipment that was built by hand, homemade signs, and bulletins that looked amateurish. It may not have looked good, but we had the Lord, each other, big dreams, and most of all, we had a simple biblical plan that was reproducible. We had 142 people show up that Sunday. Forty of them were visitors from out of the area who had come to support us. Most were my youth group kids from our previous church in Oregon.

We were encouraged, our relationships with the Lord were growing stronger with each step of faith we took. In the next year, we continued to care for our sheep. We never stopped meeting together. We were bold. Our small groups grew, and God blessed us with a few hundred new converts.

We continued to trust God for our needs. After that first year, we had grown to about five hundred people. We needed three services. The cinema we met in was having a lot of financial struggles, and we weren't sure how much longer we would be able to meet there.

We could not afford to buy or build a building, and renting was out of the question because everything was too expensive. Most of our congregants were new to the faith and just learning to trust the Lord with their finances.

We prayed, and another miracle happened. I received a call from an organization that specialized in helping growing churches and church plants. I remember the call like it was yesterday. The man said, "Hello, my name is Doug. You don't know me, but we have heard about your church. We want to fly up next week, and help you buy property, and build you a building."

I remember thinking, *You are from California and you want to buy us a building? Yeah, right. What do you really want?*

They were not kidding. One week later, they flew up and helped us purchase thirty-three acres. I wasn't thrilled about the amount of land; it seemed like way too much. The biggest church I had known had owned five acres, and that was plenty. They said that the price was right, so buy it. I wasn't thrilled about the location of the land either, but at that point I didn't care where it was, as long as we were going to have a place of our own. Later, we found out that the new high school was going in across the street. We also found out that the highway corridor would become the most sought-after land in the area, and we were right in the middle of it. Looking back, I realize that I was just along for the ride. Doug and his organization helped us design the plans for a building and get it built. I remember telling them there was no way we could pay them back. They agreed that it would take awhile. He assured me, "At some point you will be able to, and when you can, you will."

It was unbelievable! When we were six months from completion of the new building, we moved into the Post Falls Middle School gymnasium and waited for our building to be completed. I used to go into our building while it was being built and stand in awe of what God was doing.

Meanwhile, God added to our numbers daily. Finally, the new building was completed. When our church was just two years old, we had a beautiful 25,000-square-foot building. Soon after moving in, we had a new problem. Actually, it was becoming a routine issue, which kept us on our toes. After only six weeks in the new building, we grew from 850 people to 1,600. A year later we had 2,300 people in five services. In three years, God had grown His new church from four families to 2,300 people!

THE CROSSROADS

During this time, the pressure of such rapid and tremendous growth was incredible. We believed in a specific style of ministry. We had a system we all had bought into. We believed our people should be shepherded. If someone was missing, we should call. We believed in relational discipleship. When someone came to the Lord, they needed someone to walk with them; they needed to be taught. When someone was sick, we needed to be there to pray and to help.

We had always done things in small groups, because this was the only place that could provide the care we felt people needed. The truth was, we had grown so fast that the relational infrastructure we had created could not keep up. We had leaders with little support or accountability. We had people with little training. We kept rebuilding systems to support our current numbers, but by the time we were ready to implement these new structures, they were useless; the church had already outgrown them. We were always shooting at a moving target.

We were overwhelmed. The largest church any of us had ever been in was three hundred. None of us had ever done what we were doing. I had never been a senior pastor. Aaron had never led a youth group. Brandon had never been in charge of small groups. Lydia had never been a women's minister. Most of our elders had never been elders before. I can remember getting exasperated and thinking, *What in the world was God thinking?* How had we gotten ourselves into this mess? It is one thing to handle growth when you are ready to deal with it—when you have the experience and a workable plan. We were in way over our heads!

We had a value system that drove everything we did. We believed in relationship and shepherding—in discipling those we won to the Lord. We believed in seeking out the missing. I remember the last week I called *all* the families that had been missing from church that week. I made 162 phone calls. I know I looked beat when I came into the office on that Thursday.

One of the staff said, "What's up with you?" I explained I had finally called all the people and *now* I had to write a sermon. His question: "Why are you doing all of that?" I told him that a pastor is supposed to pastor his people. My co-worker said something that still sticks with me. He said, "No, your job is to make sure people are pastored. You always talk about raising up people to do what you do; now let us do what you do." Our team realized that we were at a crossroads.

Each team member had to make a decision. I was beat; our staff was exhausted. We had a choice to make. If all we looked at were the numbers, we'd say the success was killing us. But we knew in our hearts this wasn't success. We were on our way to losing. We were becoming a show.

I called in our leaders and said, "Here are our choices. There is only so much money and time. We have to make a decision. We are at a Y in the road. We can either spend our money and time creating a show in order to keep these people entertained, or we can attempt things we have never done here before." I reminded them that our success had not come because of a show; we had never had the right equipment or a full-time worship person. It had come because God blessed us in our obedience to His Word, just as He promised. From church discipline to shepherding His sheep, to raising up new leaders to pastor others, we had purposed to follow Christ's example.

Since two of our church values were to raise up leaders and to pastor our people, we had to make a decision. If we could not or would not do this anymore, then we had to change our church's purposes, which we had written on the wall and in our weekly bulletin. It had become obvious that we could not do it the way we had done it anymore.

I put the decision before them. Did they want the show, or did they want to do what we said we would do in the beginning? If we chose to continue on the course we started, it would have to be in a whole new way.

Each had to make a decision. I knew what they would choose.

We had been under a lot of pressure to become more professional on Sunday mornings. Some had wanted us to try to find ways to hire people to lead the arts and worship. They wanted us to spend a lot of money on equipment and focus on becoming like many of the large churches in the U.S.

We decided to spend money, but not in the way that some would have liked. We thought for sure that our next move would slow down the growth. We actually thought we would lose several hundred people. However, we prayed and followed the way we felt God wanted.

The next Sunday, as a leadership team we stood in front of our people and explained our dilemma. We outlined the two options, reminded them what we had believed since the beginning, and told them what choice we had made. We would not seek to be like other big churches. We honestly shared our hearts and our convictions, and we let them know we were tired and needed their help if we were to be successful in the next step.

Then, we shared the plan. We would become completely small groups driven. We would spend our money on pastors who could disciple and release, rather than hire people who focused on the worship service. We would deemphasize the show and focus on shepherding, discipleship, and relationship. We let them know they would have to step up and become ministers, not spectators—after all, this church is called Real Life Ministries (RLM), and we must all be ministers. The people went nuts. They gave us a standing ovation!

In two weeks we grew another five hundred people. "Boy, did that backfire!" we laughed. Only it really wasn't funny.

We pulled people right out of the crowd. We called them to step up and take their rightful place as ministers in the Lord's work, and they did. Now it was our job to get them trained. Again God provided. Jim and Christy Blazin were invaluable in helping us put together training for these new leaders.

We organized our congregation into smaller church communities and put a staff pastor in charge of each community. The pastor was responsible for training volunteer coaches, who would each support a handful of small group leaders. These small group leaders were trained to be *pastors* of their groups.

We then trained our people to go to their small group leaders with their problems rather than go to the staff first. The leaders would work within a support network, referring those who needed additional help to those better qualified or equipped to handle specific situations when necessary.

We concentrated on building leaders. Instead of merely feeding those who had been Christians for years but had never really grown up, we were going to force those who stuck around to grow up and serve.

We would be taking a chance. We knew that. Most of these men and women had never done anything but sit in a church pew, if they had been in church at all. Most had no training, no history of service, and certainly no experience in church leadership. We recognized that most of those we would put into leadership had only been Christians for a short time or came from a church that had taught nothing about real discipleship, but we were determined to do the unthinkable. We would release them, rather than control them. With our community structure, we would not only provide accountability for the group leaders, we would turn this group of people into an army.

A Look at the Early Church

During this time I had been reading the first few chapters of Acts in a new way. I was thinking about what starting a church must have been like for them. In the upper room, on the day of Pentecost, there were 120 people. By the end of the day 3,000 had gathered. What did the disciples do? How did they handle what must have been such utter chaos and confusion?

Some people glorify the early church instead of the Christ they represented. They say, "Wow! I wish we could be like the early church." Sometimes we forget that the early church had problems from the beginning too.

I began to look deeper. While the leaders had seen crowds during their time with Jesus, 3,000 new converts in one day must have been overwhelming and terrifying. The early church had leaders who were completely green too, leaders who had never actually led. A closer look showed people fighting about who was going to serve the widows, people vying for power, and people distorting the Scriptures. Every letter written to the new churches was written to combat confusion over gifts, salvation, or Judaism. The letters told the adults, who were acting like children, to knock it off!

The early church was organized chaos.

As I continued to study, I remember thinking, *I see us in here! We can relate to these circumstances. We understand being overwhelmed.* It gave me a picture of what we could look like. If God could use green, confused people in the first century, He could do it here and now.

We determined to keep trying and trust the Lord to lead us farther and cover our mistakes. We would pray, and the Lord would show us where we needed to be and how we needed to change. If a group leader failed, God would bring it to our awareness. If someone tried to cause division, the Holy Spirit would help us stop it. As people stepped up and inevitably made mistakes, as we all had, we would gently shepherd them. We would give them instruction and grace, dusting them off when they fell and sending them out again—wiser from the failure. When it came right down to it, what choice did we have?

We are called to lead as God defines it; it is God who makes the church grow. We hadn't manufactured anything. When we looked around, we wondered how this had happened. There was no sign in front of our building, no property along the freeway for all to notice, not even a correct address in the phone book. Our gadgets either didn't work or were handled by people who didn't really know how to use them. We had a volunteer worship leader and no full-time children's ministry person. We were plugging the holes as fast as we could.

This was clearly not a textbook church plant. God was sending people by the thousands. It was extremely humbling. We had more than five hundred first-time decisions for Jesus Christ in a year, not to mention all the recommitments.

In this little town of 10,000, within a twenty-five-mile radius of almost 100,000 people, God was growing a church—and planting *a philosophy that is reproducible*, no matter what gadgets and technology we had or didn't have.

THE ADJUSTMENTS

We knew we had to do something immediately. The first thing we did was to move out of our new building and turn it into the children's ministry area. We had outgrown it in one year. We had five services and were turning away people at the peak attendance hours. So we moved our worship services into the new high school across the street. The folks at the high school were gracious to us and broke their own six-month-limit rule because we were involved in the community and did things like provide school supplies and clothing for underprivileged kids.

We moved for many reasons. The foyer had come to resemble a mosh pit before and after services. Our children's ministry could not squeeze one more child in. It could easily take thirty minutes to park and then even longer to get *into* the building. New and unsaved people were turning around and going home. We watched them in frustration as they circled the parking lot in their cars and left. We wanted to reduce the number of weekly services because our staff was exhausted.

As our people grew in their ability to minister and lead, we felt ready to hire people who could help us in our weekend services. We hired a full-time children's minister and a worship minister.

We started construction on a bigger building. Most importantly, we trained more and more laypeople to minister in our newly developed small group structure. We later learned that what we had come up with was called the *metachurch* model. It would have been nice to know someone had already developed it.

We added one truly new component. We developed a way to track our people's attendance in services and small groups. We wanted to know that our people were okay. We called it the C.A.R.E. Tool—Caring for All, Reaching Everyone. It took cooperation from our people and a computer system that could track attendance. God provided Jack Lawlor, a talented man, to design this invaluable tool.

When I tell this story, many pastors ask, "Why would you want to call all your people when they are not there?" My response is, "Why wouldn't you?" Pastors are to shepherd their people. When a shepherd looks at the sheep, he watches the outside edges. Those in the middle are presumably okay, but it is around the edges that the wolves attack or the sheep can stray or get lost. Keeping tabs on church and small group attendance is a way to care for those who have joined our team and decided to be connected.

People don't want to be a number. People want to be loved and affirmed and trained. A good shepherd chases the strays *because he loves them.* If they get away, it won't be because he simply let them go.

Many pastors say, "There is no way I can do that with the numbers of people I have!" I have to agree, but as I had to learn, our job is to train leaders to have the heart of a shepherd. If we build up godly leaders who will pastor and disciple more leaders, together we *can* get it done.

Looking Back

As we implemented the system, our church took off again. Since then, our small groups have exploded in numbers and effectiveness. When we first began, many of our group leaders were only able to limp along, inexperienced. But every year they have become increasingly more effective in their service to the Lord.

When we first started, we put whoever we could find into leadership. Now, our leaders are coming from within the system. Our apprentices see a model to follow, and they are following and implementing our values. Our most effective small group leaders often became community coaches of six to ten small group leaders. Some have become elders in our church and others have come on staff. We just recently hired three more men, who developed in our system, to head whole communities.

God led us to start a church across the Washington border. All of the staff for this new plant, except one, came from within our system. Matt King, the senior pastor of this church, recommitted his life to Christ in our church. He started as a small group leader and is now the pastor of a church of more than one thousand.

We have made colossal mistakes, but God is in the business of making something great out of what we've broken.

Looking Ahead

Our system works on paper, but a funny thing happens when you add people to the process. I often say, "Everyone has a mouth, and wherever there is a mouth, there is a problem waiting to happen." It's important to have the expectation of always trying, not always succeeding. Despite our failures, God is amazing. Our attendance grew to more than 8,000 in eight years. After only one year in our newest building, we needed to remodel. The next year we added services, brought in portable classrooms, did a church plant, ran different locations, and started to plan for another building and more church plants.

As we have grown, we have been able to purchase some of the things that many people think a church is supposed to have—like sound equipment, a light system, computers for the staff. I am not sure if having them has been worth the trouble. In retrospect , they may have been more of a distraction. Having stuff has not increased our rate of growth, but some gadgets save time and are great conveniences, and for that I'm grateful.

I wonder if some church leader will come visit us and think, "This is not reproducible; we don't have the money for a building like this or these fancy video projectors." If they look at the surface, I am afraid they will believe this stuff is how we got where we are. They would be sorely mistaken. I am afraid at times some of our people will take pride in this stuff. They may come to expect it, to rely on it. They may begin to invite their friends to "come see our stuff. It's quite the show!" I pray that if the stuff gets in the way, the Lord will take it away.

God has indeed worked here at Real Life Ministries. He loves to use people who are clueless so He gets all the credit. It would be foolish to say this story has happened as the result of any one person. God wanted a church here and He acted. He is awesome! He is holy. He is unstoppable. All we can do is hold on and pray.

The Lord has shown us some things throughout our journey. He has shown us some principles that are reproducible. He has shown us that we don't need what many say is necessary to be a growing, thriving church. God can use uneducated, simple people who just use biblical principles of discipleship.

I am not saying that we shouldn't use gadgets if they can help, or that we should not have good worship music that is contemporary and led by skilled people. All of these things are beneficial as long as they serve the true vision of the church. I am saying that God has shown us some things that can be used to grow His church in ways that matter more than numbers can measure.

I believe a change is needed. The average church in America, as it is currently put together, is failing. This book will challenge you to rethink the box you were handed by those who taught you. As a leader, you are God's coach, and He wants to use you to lead His team to victory. This book will also challenge you to discover a "new" way to find true victory.

PART 1

FROM THE LOCKER ROOM TO THE ELDER BOARD ROOM

01

SWITCHING JERSEYS

A Pastor's Journey

My whole life had been about sports. I struggled for years to find my niche. I was hyperactive and struggled in school. We moved a lot, so I was always the new kid and struggled with having deep relationships. As a pastor's son, I struggled with faith and, consequently, with the church. But on the field, or on the mat, it was me, just me.

The ability to excel in sports came naturally for me. I had the physical capability and the internal desire to win. I always had something to prove, so every game or practice mattered to me more than it should have. I had to win. I lost everywhere else, or so it seemed to me as a child, so I had to win at something, and sports was where it could happen. Because sports seemed to be my place, coaches always had a lot of influence in my life. I admired them and listened to them when I would not listen to anyone else.

In my adolescence and beyond, I distanced myself from the things that mattered to my father. I loved him, but there comes a time in every son's life when his father's ideas and opinions don't count: if Dad says it, it probably isn't true. He would talk about the Lord all the time. Everything was a lesson.

My mom was the hardest-working woman I knew. She bore five kids (I was the oldest) within six years. Pastors' wives were busy enough, but she also worked another job at a Bible college because we were on a tight budget, which seemed typical of pastors back then. We lived in a glass house; it felt like everyone was watching us, expecting more of us than they did of anyone else.

When it came to faith, it was a mixed bag for me. I was rebellious and challenged everything from beliefs to Bible stories, with questions like, "Where did Cain's wife come from?" However, there were some perks to being the pastor's son—I usually had the inside track to a job with one church member or another.

As I spent time with church people outside of Sunday morning, I noticed a difference in the way these people acted. They used completely different words on Monday than they did on Sunday. Rarely, if at all, did I see the reality of Christ in their lives. It was an excuse for me to go farther down the road I wanted to take anyway. I started using alcohol and drugs at a young age, going the way of the prodigal son in almost every aspect of my life.

I later went off to North Idaho College in Coeur d'Alene on a wrestling scholarship. It was there that everything I had been taught at home was challenged or destroyed. To be honest, I wasn't trying to hold on all that hard. When I left home and no longer had the credible witness of my parents in my life, I began to see Christians through the world's eyes alone. I discovered a difference between the Christians I had seen and the other religions I was becoming familiar with. It seemed that people of these religions were more open and accepting, while Christians were mean, ignorant, guilt ridden, or hard-hearted to those who had made mistakes in their lives. They seemed to disagree with everyone, including those who were supposed to be on their side.

"Christianity doesn't seem to work for you," I would say to Christians who crossed my path. "Where is this power you speak of?" "You sin like me, but you pretend you don't." "Why would I want to be like you?"

Walking away from God and the church, I found myself in a world of self-gratification and addiction. I came to believe that we are the product of an unthinking evolutionary process, and my lifestyle followed suit. It was about me. Survival of the fittest was the name of the game, and I believed I was tough enough and smart enough to be the fittest.

WRESTLING WITH GOD

In college, wrestling became the place to prove I was the best. When I wasn't wrestling, I was chasing things that made me feel good. The more I did what I wanted to do, the emptier I became. Soon winning wasn't enough. Sex wasn't enough. Drinking became my escape.

It wasn't long before I had ruined every relationship in my life, leaving me desperate and alone. And it was at this time in my life that my parents, whom I had hurt time after time, became the prodigal's parent of the Scriptures. They had been waiting for me to come home, and now they reached out to me.

My first reasons for not accepting Christ had been intellectual ones, so my father sent me a book written by Josh McDowell— *Evidence That Demands a Verdict*. It challenged me to think. My father sent me books to answer my questions about evolution. At first I was skeptical about what they said, but as I questioned my professors, they had no answers to the challenges these books made. Slowly but surely, I came to believe that Christianity was based in truth.

My past became my greatest struggle. I was convinced that God could not forgive me for my long list of indiscretions. But God used my parents and some friends to extend his grace to me. I had heard the message thousands of times before, but this time I listened. It was time for me to take on my biggest problem—to quit drinking and doing drugs, the things that were controlling my life. As I started to experience God's love and help, my life changed.

Shortly after that turning point in my life, I made the decision not to date non-Christian girls anymore. I would commit every part of my life to the Lord. I believed differently than before, and I was going to live differently as well. Soon God sent a Christian young lady into my life. At a time when I was lonely and had lost many friends because partying was not a part of my life anymore, God sent Lori.

Everything was in order now that I had a relationship with God and a godly woman in my life. For the first time in a long time, I was stable. God had helped me find his grace. Lori was strong; she was an anchor that helped me find strength. As my life changed direction, God brought people to be godly friends and provide a social life that did not leave me with regret.

WRESTLING FOR GOD

I was ready to begin my assent to "God's big plan for my life": the top of the wrestling world. I would finish my college career by winning what had eluded me—a national championship—and then try to become an Olympian. Most who sought that goal failed, but I would give it my best shot. After that, my plans were to become a coach. My whole life had been about wrestling, and coaches were the kind of people I admired most. I would lead young men to individual championships and teams to state and national titles. God would take me to the top. Of course, I would give him credit for it and tell everyone what Jesus could do in them as well.

By the time I was a junior in college, I had won most of the awards a person in my sport could win. In high school, I had been a part of state championships in multiple sports and a three-time state champion in wrestling. During college, I was on multiple national championship wrestling teams and placed in the top four in the nation three times and in the top two twice, which made me a college All-American.

I had given my life to Christ but was dead set against ever following my father into the ministry. I had seen far too many hurtful things within the walls of a church building to want to do that to myself, to Lori, or to my future children. Although I had faith in Jesus after many years of internal battle, I had no faith in the church, no faith in people.

The summer before my junior year, Lori and I married and moved to a little college in the middle of Montana. Yes, in the middle of nowhere. I achieved personal success there, but the move was hard for my wife. While I was chasing my dream, she was sitting in a podunk town with few friends. So, for my senior year we moved to a larger college near my parents and nearer to people Lori could relate to.

The college I transferred to had just hired a potential Olympian as an assistant coach. Instead of my finding help from a coach whose goal is to bring out the best in his athletes, I ran into my first experience with a bad coach. Oh, I had had coaches who did not know a lot about the sport they were coaching but never one who did not care about me as a person. I found out quickly that I was a part of this coach's plan to achieve personal success for himself. I became an object to be used rather than a person to be developed.

The problems did not stop there. I had always been on teams with committed coaches and athletes, everyone working together for individual greatness and team glory, but what I found there were people who had no desire or passion to win. They liked the idea of winning but were not ready to be committed to what it takes. These coaches and wrestlers were interested in the sport but not the lifestyle it required. Few were wholeheartedly committed, including the coaches. Few thought beyond the next big party, in season or out. I had given up that mentality, as it had ruined my earlier life and kept me from attaining any worthwhile goal. These people seemed to be enamored with mediocrity, and I had nothing in common with that. The painful realization hit me that I was on my own, with no experience that would help me succeed on this kind of team.

IT ALL COMES APART

As I was dealing with my new team, Lori and I were getting settled into our new life. We were living in married student housing just down the street from the college. We decided we needed to get involved with other Christian people. My father had always leaned on me to get plugged in to a church, but that was tough for me. Christians made me nervous. Again, I had found faith in Jesus but did not trust Christian people. It also had been tough for me to find a church in the past year because the team traveled on the weekends to tournaments. My father, always pestering me about this, called one night to inform me that a new church plant was meeting right down the street in the college auditorium. I reluctantly agreed to check it out.

I knew my wife needed Christian friends, so we decided to start attending. As we got involved, it was a mixed bag. Although I was pretty rough around the edges and was used to being around tough people, these church people were okay. But it was really an adjustment for me. I could see my wife was happier as she found some friends she had something in common with. As we settled in, my wrestling career started to come apart around my ears. For the first time I started having problems with depression. The move had been good for my wife and for my spiritual life, but it was really, really bad for my wrestling career and my future plans.

My teammates and coaches had little interest in doing more than the bare minimum. I was struggling to get my weight down, and the attitude of my new team was affecting me. To top it off, I became physically ill, contracting a form of mono, and my dream of being a four-time All-American was in jeopardy.

Meanwhile, the inevitable happened at the church we attended. Not long after I reluctantly stepped out to get involved, internal battles in the church became evident. I remember thinking, *Here we go again*. Just what I thought would happen did happen. My reaction was, *It's cool. I was getting bored anyway. I can just be a Christian without church.*

I called my dad to gloat with the proverbial "I told you so." Instead of responding the way I anticipated, my dad said something I will never forget: "Jim, I think you should get involved there and let the Lord use your abilities to fix some of the problems rather than point at them."

I was flabbergasted! "You want me to get involved in this mess?" I had nothing to offer the church, even if I wanted to help. What could I do, teach them to wrestle? Great! Then they would know how to hurt each other physically too.

My father had always wanted me to follow in his footsteps. He believed that leading a church was the most important thing a person could do. "Dad," I said, "I will never be a pastor. No way are you sucking me into this church thing of yours." He assured me that he wasn't trying to turn me into a pastor; he just felt that every Christian was to use their gifts for the Lord. He asked me to pray about it with Lori. I remember thinking he was crazy.

MY FIRST MINISTRY

The next week something happened that forever changed the course of my life. Lori and I were walking out the door after the service, and one of the pastors came over to shake my hand. I was courteous but wanted to head home to watch a football game. He said, "Jim, I know that you have been attending for a while, and I want you to think about something. I want you to consider leading a Bible study for a few of our youth kids." There were four junior high and high school kids in the church, and no one near their age to lead them. As a young church, they could not afford to hire a youth minister. He thought Lori and I were the right age and would be great for the volunteer position. He believed that I would relate well to them, and that they would respect someone like me.

My immediate response was "No thanks." Walking out of the church, I thought, *There is no way I have time for that.* The wrestling schedule was getting ready to start, and training had to be a top priority. I told Lori that with all the problems on the team, I had to be focused. I was on my own, and besides, I had all but decided not even to attend church myself anymore.

That night my father called. "I have been thinking a lot about what you said. Jim, I want to give you an analogy I have been reflecting on. A healthy lake has water coming in and water going out. If no water continuously comes in, then the lake dries up. If a lake has water coming in but no water going out, then the lake floods and kills everything around it."

He went on to say, "Jim, God has poured so much into you. He saved you, though you were in a huge mess. He helped you with your drinking, He gave you a godly wife, He gave you salvation, but you have taken it all in and not given anything back. You will be like that lake, flooding and killing everything around you. Or you will step back from the church and have no water coming in, and you will dry up. You have choices to make, Jim. God is asking you to give. Instead of pointing out all the blemishes on His bride, the church, I believe God wants to use you to help clean her up." He told me to really pray about what God would have me do. "If you really pray, God will answer."

I sat quietly and listened. As he was speaking, my mind was racing: How would I know when God answers? Just about then, Dad answered that very question. "Jim, God will open a door. You go through when He does." When he had finished, I told him about what happened at church, and he said, "There is your answer, Jim. God is asking you to join Him. I think you should pray about it."

Lori and I did pray, and we agreed we would lead this little study with four kids for three months. Our first meeting was one I'll never forget. I had wrestled in front of thousands, had played in front of packed stands, but nothing touched the fear I felt before that first meeting. I kept it short and then, heeding Lori's advice ("You can't lose with Dairy Queen!"), took the kids out for ice cream.

The first week the four kids came to our house, the second week there were eight. After a month, my wife and I had twenty-three kids meeting in our little apartment. It was getting expensive to take all these kids to DQ every week, but to my surprise I was having the time of my life.

BECOMING A DIFFERENT GUY

Meanwhile my wrestling career was in a tailspin. For the first time, I was having a hard time enjoying it. The lack of relationship on the team, the lack of teamwork, the weight cutting—all of it was getting really hard. After losing a few matches I should have won, my confidence was waning. Furthermore, my married life and my spiritual life were changing me. For so long I had wrestled because it was all I had: my value was on the line every time I stepped onto that mat. It was who I was. Losing was not an option. If I lost, what good was I? As the Lord worked in my life and as the unconditional love of my God and my wife worked on me, wrestling started to change for me. It became something I did rather than my identity. Don't get me wrong—I wanted to win. But an internal battle was raging. Why had I wanted to win so badly? Was wrestling really that important? Was it really the sum total of Jim Putman?

Reflecting back on my last year of wrestling, I can see what God was doing. It makes sense to me now, but at the time it was the most painful experience of my life. No matter what I did, when it came to wrestling, I could not pull out of the nosedive. My life plans were crumbling. At the same time, I was experiencing a joy I had not felt in athletics. I was still fighting, but for something different. I was fighting for the lives of kids. The kids were changing and growing, the youth group was exploding, and I was being led to a crossroads. The Lord had already set the stage for the direction He had mapped out for me to take.

My wrestling career came to an end at the 1991 national championships: a three-time college All-American and a two-time finalist was out of the tournament without even placing. It was unheard of. For six months after that, whenever I smelled a wrestling mat, I felt like throwing up.

God had let me down, I thought. All my dreams were shattered, and everything I had done was a waste. My plans to go further in wrestling were gone, at least in my mind. I had almost completed a four-year degree in history/teaching and planned to be a coach after pursuing my dream of making the Olympic team. But now all that remained was finishing my degree and finding a coaching job somewhere. I finished up my student teaching and took a job as a head coach at a local high school. I endured the teaching in the classroom and enjoyed the coaching on the mat, but at the same time I felt really alive when I worked with the kids in the church youth group.

MORE CHANGES

The next big change in my life came after about a year of working with the youth group kids. It was time to find a permanent coaching and teaching position. The youth group was growing past my ability to handle it on a part-time basis. I had to make some decisions. The pastor knew I was at a real crossroads, and he approached me about taking a position as the full-time youth pastor, which they could now afford because the church had grown. I told him that I had poured too much time into the teaching thing to just walk away from it. Besides, I wasn't qualified to be a pastor anyway. I loved working with kids, but it would have to be as a volunteer.

I started putting together my résumé and making calls to high schools and colleges that might need a coach. Near the end of the semester at the school where I was student teaching, something happened that led me to the biggest unexpected course change in my young life.

There was a girl in one of my junior high social studies classes. She had started the semester as a vibrant, funny young lady who was a joy to have in class. As the semester went on, she had changed.

One Tuesday I asked her to stay after class. She slumped in her chair with more attitude than normal. After the rest of the students had shuffled out of the classroom, I started in. "I don't know what has happened, but you have changed. You were one of my favorite students. You lit up the room with your personality. I don't know what is going on, but I'd like to help if I can."

She stared at the floor and then began to cry. She slowly explained that during her younger childhood her father had a problem with drinking. Though he had been sober for a while, he had started drinking again. Her parents had started partying, and she had to become the parent to her many siblings. She alluded to some other things happening but would not elaborate. The apprehensive look on her face told me that there was more to the story than she wanted to share with me. I told her that I cared about her and that I would see what I could do to help.

At that moment I made a decision that would not be popular with the school leadership. Even back then, Christian teachers were told not to share their faith. But this girl needed more than a schoolteacher going by the book could give her. I told her that I could do nothing about her parents except to report it, but then I shared my faith with her, telling her that there was one who would love her just as she was, and that God had a plan for her life. She listened. I prayed with her and invited her to our church youth group.

That night I worried that I had shared too much. The next morning I reported to the principal what had happened. He explained that he had already received a call from the girl's mother. She was very upset that a teacher would talk to her daughter about Christianity. The principal told me that I could not speak about Jesus, or our church activities, when dealing with the kids. I sat quietly for a moment and then asked him if he knew what was happening in the girl's home. The principal said he did, and he admitted that it was not healthy. I asked him a question that had been lingering in my mind all night: "Sir, could you tell me what good knowing about Christopher Columbus is going to do for that girl?"

As I asked the question and listened to his explanation, it occurred to me that this question had affected me far more than it had him.

There comes a time in each of our lives when we are challenged to evaluate our convictions. Teaching in a public school is a very valuable career, and Christian schoolteachers can make an impact on their students even as silent witnesses. But for me, right then, I knew that my teaching had to be about something that made an eternal difference.

I had been shaped for a different purpose. God had led me to a place I swore I would never go. If I was to coach wrestling or anything else, it had to ultimately end in a conversation about eternity. I had to be a pastor.

BECOMING A COACH FOR GOD'S TEAM

That night as I told my wife what had happened, we both knew our lives would change forever. After praying with Lori, I called the pastor and told him that I had changed my mind and that God had made it clear to me He wanted me to be a pastor. He wanted me to be a coach for *His* team.

In the years since then, I have coached one kind of sports team or another. Though most of my career has been in the church, I enjoyed working in the public school system as well as being a head coach, coaching several state champions, and coaching teams to championships. Here at Real Life, we have even started a kids' wrestling program.

However, God has led me to pour my life into a different kind of team. I now get the opportunity to coach one of God's teams. My job is to develop God's players, to achieve God's objectives. We now fight against God's enemies. In this battle, losing has bigger consequences than just unhappy fans or athletic directors.

As I made the transition from sports to ministry, I must admit that my expectations were still to win. I had had success in coaching sports teams, so coaching God's team had to be a piece of cake. *It's*

God's team, these are God's people, I thought. As I traded in the mats and ball fields for the church boardrooms, I found something I did not expect. I found people who not only couldn't play together but didn't know how to play at all—a losing team. Over the years, it's been disappointing to see God's teams (the church) all over the country doing things that a good high school or college coach would never allow on a sports field. Many of God's teams have created playbooks that were not approved by The Coach, and as a result we have lost more than we should have.

02

CHASING A DREAM

Looking for the Winning Church

Imagine that a coach named Joe just received a call from the owner of a professional football team. The owner offers him the chance of a lifetime—to coach a team in the National Football League. Joe has loved and played football for as long as he can remember; he has studied the best players, the best coaches, and the best strategies. He has put his time into developing his skills as a coach and proving he knew what he was talking about by winning in every program he led. He had prayed for this opportunity, and finally it had arrived.

Without asking for details, Joe immediately says, "Yes!" In his mind the money doesn't matter, because he simply loves the game. This is his dream. He makes the trip to meet the owners, the general manager, and the president of operations. They seem competent and committed. They assure him they will provide what he needs to win. They will support whatever changes he needs to make. The bottom line: win as soon and as much as possible. The team Joe has been asked to coach hasn't been horrible, but even if they were, it wouldn't have mattered. He just wanted the opportunity to prove himself, and this is it. This is the chance he had been praying for. So he's off and running, ready and excited.

As Joe heads to the office for his first day of work, he is as excited as a little kid when he walks into the team complex. The dream, however, of being a coach is soon overshadowed by the stark reality of the work and the details involved.

Joe starts the day investigating what has gone wrong with this team in the past. As he looks at the assistants' résumés, he realizes they are a talented group. Some of them are more qualified than he is: high school Coach of the Year awards, college assistants, head coaches, and even some ex-professional coaches. He's impressed and maybe even a little intimidated. However, as he interviews them, he quickly sees there are problems.

First, these coaches are talented and knowledgeable, but they all have different philosophies about how to play and win. As a result of these different views, they have different ideas about how the team needs to be reshaped. Secondly, there is an obvious relational rift between at least three of the men on the staff. They don't know each other well, let alone want to spend time together. Thirdly, as Joe starts to question the coaches, he discovers they're all in agreement on one thing: the owners will not let them do their jobs. They undercut the staff and have differing views of what's right and wrong. They jump into many situations without understanding what is really going on, and in many cases, they make things more difficult. In other words, there is a power struggle going on that is affecting the team before the players even hit the field.

The organization has no agreed-upon goals. They disagree about who's to blame for mistakes and who's to receive credit when things are done well. These leaders don't agree on personnel, strategy, or philosophy. They don't even define winning the same way. To make matters worse, there are secret alliances between some coaches and the owner, and between coaches and some of the star players. Special treatment is given, which has affected the team chemistry.

At best, the results of the first day's meetings are discouraging, and Joe can't imagine what the meetings with the players will look like.

The next day he wakes up less enthusiastic, but he is tough and he moves on because this is his big chance, this is his dream. He starts the day with meetings with key players, and his worst fears are confirmed. The lack of teamwork among the leadership has the players' confidence in the front office and coaching staff at zero.

There's no cohesion among the players. How could there be? Several follow one coach, hating the others, while some players would like to be traded. Others just want to prove themselves in their given area and then move on to a big contract on a different "winning team." Some have decided their personal glory is more important than team accomplishments. A few have just given up on winning altogether; they believe it is a lost cause.

The anger runs deep—blaming has become an expertise. The offense hates the defense and vice versa; both blame the other for the many losses. The concept of winning with consistency is a fantasy, and no one on the team believes it can be done. Joe hasn't been here long, but he is already so discouraged that he wants to spend a little time alone. So he decides to watch the team films in his office. No surprise that as he watches, he sees the attitudes and beliefs of players and coaches taking form in the game. People miss blocks, jump offside, run the wrong plays; there's a lack of discipline. At the end of the game, they lose. The saddest thing for the coach is to see enough talent on his team to win, but they don't. The result: fewer people in the stands. This especially frustrates the owners—a losing team doesn't pay its bills. The owners want results, but there's no way Joe can give it to them when they're a part of the problem.

REALITY CHECK

My own experience in the church was very similar to this story. Since I had little experience as a leader in the church, I thought it would be easy to coach God's team. I mean, God had built His team to win, hadn't He? I was working with Spirit-filled Christians, not the hardheaded athletes I had dealt with in my past. There were no Bible college classes to teach me about what I would find, and to say that I was surprised by what I found would be an understatement. My own past experience in churches wasn't positive. But it couldn't look as bad on the inside as it did to a non-Christian wanting to find blemishes on the outside—could it?

I believed that I had worked through my toughest experiences already to prepare me for the new team—the church. It ought to be easy, and even if it wasn't, I was used to working hard and finding a way to win. Surely it couldn't be any tougher than leading a sports team to a championship. So, I took that determined coaching mind-set that had helped me win in the past into my first ministry experiences. As I got into my new team's locker room (board room) and saw what was happening, I was discouraged beyond words.

Like Joe's story, I walked into a nightmare. When I became a youth minister, I was tempted to quit soon after starting. This new team I was to help coach was anything but a team. As a new leader I was required to attend leadership meetings. My first elders' meeting was a microcosm of the dysfunction I found almost everywhere. Our meetings had little to do with reaching the world for Jesus. The leaders seemed more concerned about who was going to shampoo the carpet, or who would talk to Mr. Jones, who was upset that the Christian flag was on the left side of the sanctuary instead of the right. The worship was too loud or too old or too new; the sermon was too long, or too shallow, or too deep.

As I listened, I realized that these people, though they loved God, were not a team with a mission. They didn't have a common view of what winning even was. They were not in agreement about where to go, so they were not going anywhere. As near as I could tell by their conversations and actions, their goal was to keep their people comfortable.

When the pastor tried to direct the men to a goal, it was like herding cats. Needless to say, I found this frustrating. The elders were like backseat drivers who would question our every move. Every decision was under scrutiny.

When it came to staff relationships, there weren't any. We worked at the same building, but we didn't know each other and were certainly not going in the same direction. Each person had their own little department. As a result of the problems within the leadership, there were factions everywhere within the congregation—all blaming the other for the church's lack of growth.

Due to the unstable leadership, no one was ready to take a chance, to change or do what needed to be done to win. If a chance was taken, it had to work immediately or it was the wrong decision, signaled by the familiar comment "I told you so." Even worse, the majority of people in the church stopped believing that something could be done about it. It had been an empty experience for so long that no one had any fire for the work. With no vision, the people had stopped moving toward anything meaningful; rather than fighting the enemy, we were fighting each other. I think the worst thing was to see that people just didn't seem to care anymore. There was this sense of complacency that permeated every aspect of the church.

As a youth minister, I did not have the power to make any changes. What seemed obviously wrong to me was just the way it was. But I was impatient. I would circumvent the leadership, figuring it was easier to say I was sorry than to get permission. I couldn't help the church as a whole, so I would do my own thing with the youth group. I burned bridges I shouldn't have burned, and as a result I lost some ability to help because of a lack of credibility. After hitting many roadblocks—some my fault, some the fault of others—I decided to look around and find someone in my area who was succeeding.

LOOKING FOR A DIFFERENT WAY

I set out to learn from the pastors of churches in my community who had no doubt dealt with such things much longer. I needed some advice from an experienced coach. My constant question was, how do I help change things? Surely there had to be a coach nearby who had learned to navigate this new obstacle course God had led me into. I was relieved to find that I wasn't the only one who had dealt with these issues.

Those who had recognized the problem had fought many losing battles. Many around my town had lost but were still fighting. I found committed coaches all around me, but few who had successfully led their team to what they or I would call a spiritual team championship.

Some of the coaches I met with had given up altogether and were biding their time, waiting to retire. They were not conquering the enemy, battling in the trenches for the souls of men; they were just surviving. Many a well-meaning pastor told me that I was far too idealistic. They had once been that idealistic, but they had learned what I would learn soon enough—to lower my expectations. Many of the younger ambitious pastors were using their churches as stepping-stones to other, bigger ministries. It was a career for them and they wanted to reach the top. Oh yes, it was about God, but there was a whole lot of "them" in there as well.

Those conversations forced me to face my own pride. They caused me to deal with my own motivations for success. As I listened, I realized that the church was not just losing where I lived, but it was losing in most of the churches in the area where I lived. As I looked in the locker room of God's team, I found a mess.

I did what is natural for a young pastor. I started looking for a coach of a "winning" church to talk with. If a church was growing numerically, I believed this was an automatic indication that the church was winning and that the coach must be a coach worth listening to.

After lengthy conversations with some of these pastors, I quickly discerned that my view of winning was different from theirs. I heard a lot about numbers and formulas and buildings and radio programs, and I came to rethink my view of numerical growth. Now, I have no problem with numbers. I have found that numbers can be an indicator that a team is winning. Jesus cared about numbers. He came to reach the masses; He wishes none to be lost. But winning is not necessarily numbers. As a non-Christian, I had heard a lot of people claim to be Christian, but few seemed to have something I actually wanted. I had come to understand that many go to church, but going to church is not the same thing as following Jesus. I didn't want to be a part of a place that just gathered a crowd.

As I spoke with many of the pastors of bigger churches, I noticed they were often proud of their well-equipped auditoriums or their huge parking lots. They were excited about how many they had in church last Sunday and were eager to give me a tape or CD of their last sermon. However, I did not hear how their people were serving or witnessing, how many decisions for Christ they were seeing, or how they were training people for ministry. I didn't hear about relationships. I heard a lot about the show on the weekend, how to use video projectors, or how to tweak the worship service to really draw a crowd. The buildings I visited were probably full on the weekend, but they were like cemeteries during the week. As I walked away from those many meetings, I once again believed that the team was losing in most places. Even in many churches that appeared to be winning, we were getting drilled.

As I became familiar with the inner workings of church, I became more discouraged. I had started this church thing to help change the way the world looked at Jesus by changing the way they looked at the church. I knew the only way to do that was to be a part of the solution rather than just pointing at the problem. (My dad had said that to me so often it had become a mantra for me.)

I wanted God to use me to help the church be something that God would be proud of. Now I realized that I had more questions than answers. I knew that what the church was doing wasn't working, but I still had no idea what would work. I wanted to know if what I was seeing around me was unique or if the church was in this much trouble all over the U.S. I began to read all I could about the church, and because I was a sports fan, stats made sense to me.

03

AND THE SCOREBOARD SAYS . . .

How Are We Doing?

I have come to realize that my personal adolescent hang-ups with Jesus were not a problem with Him but with Christians in the church. Sadly, most churches today are not representing Christ well.

It seems we have come to believe we can love Jesus yet hate His church. Maybe "hate" is too strong a word, but many certainly do not love the church or believe it has any relevance in their lives. Christians in America have come to believe in an individualistic kind of relationship with God. We say, "I love God, but church is something I go to if I have time."

Why do they feel this way? George Barna, a Christian pollster who researches the church in America, sheds some light on the matter. His group has found that an incredibly small number of people expect to have an experience with God at church. Not only do people who attend church in America think they won't grow from the experience, most don't believe that the church can do anything corporately that will cause much of a stir in the community they live in. There is good reason for that, I guess. Most churches do not typically do anything in the towns they live in.

When I was deciding whether to go into the ministry, I struggled with my own feelings about the church. I wondered if I would be wasting my life on a lost cause. I also felt that I was unqualified to lead in the church because of my lack of seminary training. It was not until I understood what the church was that I felt like I had something to contribute.

SO WHAT IS A CHURCH?

As I am sure you have noticed already, I believe that the church is supposed to be a collection of transformed individuals molded by God *into a team*. I see teams and teamwork everywhere in Scripture. In fact, I don't believe a person is a mature Christian unless they are a part of Christ's mission to reach the world through His team—the church. I don't care how much Scripture they know or how many seminary degrees they have, they are not in the will of God, thus not a mature believer, unless they are a part of His team—the church. The Christian life is a team sport.

I have seen many who play a team sport but think only as individuals. People like this may have a good game as players, but the team loses because the players care little about the team. They may act as though they have won something, but they haven't. This game we play cannot be won without a team.

GOD'S DEFINITION OF A CHURCH

When I say these kinds of things, people ask me how I define the word *church*. When I speak of church, I mean a body of believers working as individuals and together as a team to achieve the Lord's goals. God's plan is to glorify Himself through this team. As individuals we minister wherever we work and live. We use our talents, gifts, and resources to minister in our communities in ways that can be done only as a collective force. Our winning team reaches the world with the message of the gospel and then disciples those who have been won to obedience and replication.

Some try to get out of being involved in a local church by claiming they are a part of the global church through a parachurch organization or a feed-the-children program. I have no problem with those extracurricular activities, but again I believe that all believers are to be molded into a local team for God's purposes. It's great that so many minister around the world through missions, but I believe God wants a presence in every town. I believe the local church is God's vehicle for reaching the world one person, one town, at a time.

As is mandated in the Scriptures, a church is to have a plurality of leaders who are appointed in every town. The Bible calls them elders; I call them coaches (see Titus 1:5). They must meet the leadership requirements mandated in Scripture and have a desire to fulfill their responsibility to the Lord and His team. Often, men want the title and benefits that come with leadership without the responsibility and sacrifice.

When I explain what the church is, some say, "Well then, a small group can be a church." I agree, it can be, but a lot of small groups working together with accountability, organization, and good coaching can do more for the kingdom than one small group can. A team of focused and organized people in a local area can do something together for and with God that could not be done as individuals or even as a small group.

Although some argue that a building can become an idol, a place we attend instead of a body of believers with a purpose, let's not swing the pendulum too far. I have been a pastor with a building and a pastor without one. The building can become a tool, used in the right hands, to change a community. A building can be used to do some damage to the enemy in the town you live in.

DEFINING TERMS: WHAT IS WINNING?

During a game, coaches and players are constantly looking at the scoreboard. They want to know what the score is because game strategy changes based on that tally. If their team falls behind, they double their efforts and change the game plan. As the clock winds down, those on the losing team become more desperate. The intensity heightens during the last few minutes of the game.

How is God's team in the United States doing in these last days? As the clock runs down and we look at the scoreboard, what do we see? As a church, what are we trying to accomplish? How do we score? What *is* winning? Are we ahead, behind, or tied?

Just as Scripture reveals how a team is to work, it also reveals what winning is. The Bible lays out the field for us—the physical and spiritual world we live in. We find out that there is a purpose to this game we play. We discover where we came from, why we live, where we are going, what rules we play by , and how we win.

We find that God's desire was to spend time on this field with the creatures He created. God desired a relationship with humans, so He gave us a choice. Relationship can only happen when choice is given. He warned us that sin would be tantamount to saying, "I don't trust You, God. I don't want what You want. I don't want to be in relationship with You." To reject God is to say "I want to be my own God." The result of rejecting God as Lord and walking away from relationship with our creator and sustainer is like unplugging our cell phone from the battery charger. We can run for a while, but eventually we will die.

God's rulebook, the Bible, explains that we play this game against an evil opponent whose method is deception and whose desire is our complete destruction. The Scriptures reveal in 1 John 5 that

God has been on a mission to save us since man fell into the hands of this enemy. The Word tells us that God so loved the world that He desired a relationship with us in spite of our sin (see John 3:16). The entirety of the Scriptures reveals this game and how to play to win.

For those of us who have accepted Jesus as Lord and Savior, we now understand life on this planet in a whole new way. Because we understand His love and are thankful for it, we have been given the privilege of joining Him on His mission to save the world (see Galatians 2; 2 Cor. 5:18–20). In sports terminology, He bought our contract for the highest possible price and made us a part of His team. Before we can play, we must be developed through a discipleship process that helps us understand our mission, play this new game, and be successful in our position on the team.

Jesus will always take us as we are, but He will not leave us that way. He will start the process of unmaking what we have become so that He can remake us into something useful for His purposes. God's plan was to disciple us through the Word, through His Spirit, and with the guidance of His coaches. In this discipleship process, He gives us teachers (coaches) who will help us understand what it means to follow Him. He also gives us His Word as a guidebook so that we can understand the game. He gives us teammates who help us win this game that can only be won as a team. He gives us the Holy Spirit who guides us into His perspective of life and eternity. He gives us His heart to care about what He cares about, his eyes to see what He sees, and His power to do what He would have us do.

As we grow in Him, we move from self-serving, thoughtless, hard-hearted beings into the players God wants us to become. We are now able to become one with other believers to form His team. Yes, we play as individuals and as a team as well. God has given each person gifts and talents for the purpose of using them for this team. The result of the discipleship process is people who can serve God wherever they work or play as a part of His team.

THE MISSION REVEALED

The mission is explained in Matthew 28. The Lord tells His disciples to go into the world and make disciples. This process has a beginning point, an entry point, so to speak. We then enter into the developmental stage where we are taught the rules of the game and we learn to obey them. We are taught that we have a place on a team, and we learn to work with others. Finally, there is a releasing point, where we allow our trained players to play and even become coaches themselves.

So what is winning? Many think winning is about numbers. We want converts, they say. Wrong! Winning is making disciples—converts who are discipled onto God's team and taught to take part in Christ's mission. Numbers don't mean much unless you are counting the number of people being transformed by the Holy Spirit. Disciples are those able to stand up under the pressure of the world. They are able to share their faith unashamed. They are filled with the fruit of the Spirit, which results in increased relationship with others and glory to God.

THE SCORE IN THE UNITED STATES

A few years ago I attended a major mission conference that both inspired and depressed me. All of the most influential mission organizations came together to figure out how to reach parts of the world that had never heard about Jesus. They had amazing speakers who had been committed for years to reaching the world for Jesus. Many of my heroes were involved, men who had not only talked a good game but for many years led their teams to victory. The goal was to get churches excited about missions, and they were doing a good job.

One speaker, a pastor of a successful church that had sent many missionaries into the world, said something that disturbed me for weeks: "The American church is like a flower. For many years it was the most beautiful of all flowers. It bloomed and grew for all to see. But as we all know, the flower has been dying. The flower is not what it used to be, but don't fear. Just before a flower dies, it accomplishes its most important task. It casts its seed." He went on to say that we have the opportunity as pastors to be a part of a very important thing. We can guide our churches to help cast our seed to foreign lands where the seed is being accepted and is growing. We have the opportunity to take our resources of money, people, and time, and focus them where the gospel is working.

As I listened, I began to struggle. He seemed to be saying, just give up on America and the American church because we all know it isn't winning. Though I did not agree with his conclusion, he was admitting what many who have researched the church had discovered: *We are losing!*

Many studies these days measure the church's effectiveness in culture. The numbers are shocking. According to the Barna Research Group, there are about 360,000 churches in America. Current numbers tell us that only 15 percent of these churches are growing, and only 2 to 5 percent of the churches are experiencing new conversion growth. I interpret that to mean most of the churches in America are losing. Those that are growing are doing so by transfer growth. This means that a small percentage of the bigger churches are getting bigger and the smaller churches are shrinking or disappearing altogether. We are merely reshuffling the deck with the same cards.

In that same study we also find that 50 percent of all evangelical churches in America did not have a single convert last year. We gain a little and we lose a lot. The death rate of elderly Christians accounts for some of this. The bigger contributor is a wide-open back door—we are losing people faster than we are gaining them.

The statistic that breaks my heart is the one Josh McDowell gives in his book *The Last Christian Generation*. In it he reveals that 85 percent of kids who come from Christian homes do not have a biblical worldview. Most of them are leaving the faith between ages eighteen and twenty-four, never to return. Many of the churches that do give their conversion numbers every year are usually giving the number of children that were baptized from their already-Christian congregations. Now we find that those young converts do not make it past their eighteenth birthday when it comes to their faith.[1]

While we are losing people, other religions are growing. Islam is the fastest-growing religion in the world and is growing rapidly in the U.S. in spite of 9/11. Mormonism is the fastest-growing religion in America. Eastern philosophy permeates our society and has invaded every part of our thinking. The new American religion is one of no wrongs and everyone going to heaven. It is a hodge-podge of multiple religions, with the main objective being self-fulfillment and satisfaction. The Christian world has incorporated many of the doctrines of these religions without even knowing it. God's winning team was supposed to reach the world. Instead, the world is reaching us.

When the unchurched are asked why they don't go to a church, most say they don't because they have not been asked. What in the world is happening? Barna reports that most Christians will die without ever sharing their faith with anyone else. It makes sense when you remember what the culture is teaching: "What is good for you is good for you and what is good for me is good for me. Why does it matter if you believe my thing or your thing when everything leads to the same place?"

You can see the loss of the church's influence everywhere. We lament this fact at election time or when the Supreme Court makes another bad decision, but our Christian people do little to help matters. Some believers get sidetracked into believing if we change the laws, America will be godly again. But you cannot mandate morality. Christians could change the world by committing themselves to the mission Jesus gave us. If we lived and loved, and shared our faith the way Jesus asked us to, we would have a chance to see real transformation in the hearts of men and women. If we change the hearts, we change the votes people cast.

If we look closely at the scoreboard, it tells us that the church in the United States is losing badly.

---

1. Josh McDowell, *The Last Christian Generation* (Holiday, FL: Green Key, 2006), 14.

CONVERTS OR DISCIPLES?

The second part of the Lord's job description for the church is also found in Matthew 28. We are told to teach those we baptize to obey all that is commanded. First we make converts, secondly we make disciples. So how is the team doing with those who have been converted? How is the church doing with those who are supposed to be Christians? When you look at the statistics for those who do go to church, you will see very little statistical difference between the churched and the unchurched when it comes to giving, the divorce rate, and views on morality. While part of the battle may be getting them to church, the greater task lies in what to do with them once they come to church.

George Barna and his research group conducted a study of the beliefs of Christians to discover whether American Christians have a biblical worldview—one that sees the world through doctrinally sound beliefs. They asked eight simple questions, such as "Are you saved by grace through faith?" "Did Jesus have a sinless nature?" "Is there a real heaven and hell?" "Is there an absolute right and wrong?" Only 51 percent of pastors questioned had a biblical worldview.[2]

This does not surprise me, but what did surprise me was what came next in the study. Barna went to people in the congregations of those pastors who *did* have a biblical worldview and asked the same questions. Less than one in seven had a biblical worldview. In other words, though the pastor believed and taught biblical truths, the congregation did not share those views.

Our churches' families have been sucked into the media storm. Hollywood defines love, sex, and marriage. This matters because our kids spend more time watching television than they spend with the ones who are to define these words for them: their parents. Our colleges convince us that we are a product of natural processes and that the Bible is filled with myths. Our people don't know the Bible

2. "Only Half of Protestant Pastors Have a Biblical World View," *The Barna Update* (January 12, 2004); http://www.barna.org/FlexPage.aspx?Page=BarnaUpdate&BarnaUpdateID =156.

from the Koran, and if you define success as changed lives, holy living, loving God and others, sharing our faith with lost people, then the score is lopsided and we are losing.

Let's sum up what we see on the scoreboard. As we look at what is being produced in America's churches, I see nothing like what was intended by our Lord. American Christians are not on a mission. They look far more like the world than they should. They live the same way and chase the same things. Their marriages and families look the same. They are biblically illiterate and care little about sharing their faith with others. Churches are producing people who do not and cannot share the gospel. You tell me, how are we doing? What's the score?

We are losing, not everywhere, but in enough places to say there is a problem. Unless we recognize we are losing and decide to call it what it is, we will not change. We have to decide how badly we want to win. Will we do whatever it takes? Are we too comfortable with our way of doing things to change? Are we afraid to change because we don't know how? Are we motivated by the cost of losing?

Our enemy is on a seek-and-destroy mission. We're in a spiritual battle, and at the moment, we're losing. We have to make a choice to begin again and fix the problem! I believe the answer to the problem starts with the leadership. It starts with those who are called to be pastors and leaders—the coaches for God's team.

PART 2

COACHING GOD'S
CHAMPIONSHIP
TEAM

04

Mission Possible

God's Team Can and Should Win

Imagine for a moment that you built a muscle car in your garage. You spent hours building, tinkering, sanding, and painting it until it was beautiful. Not only was it beautiful, you spared no expense to make the engine as powerful as they come; you built it to go 200 miles per hour. When it came time to bring it out for a test drive, you took it out to a safe country road, and you punched it—pedal to the metal!

To your surprise, you topped out at 45 miles per hour. All that expense, all that sacrifice of your time, working on your days off, in the evenings, at times even at the expense of your family time. You knew something was wrong. This car was not doing what you built it to do. As you drove down the road, 10 mph under the speed limit, you told yourself, "Well, at least it's beautiful."

Does that sound right? No, I believe you would be filled with consternation and frustration. You would do whatever it took to figure out how to get it to do what you designed it to do.

In the same way, God designed the church to do certain things. It is supposed to look and drive a specific way. I believe God is frustrated when what He designed is not working as it should. Many pastors tell me stories about their churches, about the fights and the little progress they have made amongst the lost in the world—and they know there must be something more. They did not commit their lives to Christ and his work with this quagmire as their goal and dream. They knew they were in for a fight when they accepted the call to battle as one of God's team captains. They expected to come off the bench and get banged up—but the pain is worth it when you win. Many church leaders didn't expect to be trapped in a losing battle. Unfortunately, there are other pastors who seem to be just fine with little progress. For them, pastoring has become a career where they receive a paycheck, not a cause worth giving everything for.

I wonder if God is fine with how things are going. I wonder if the designer of the car, so to speak, is happy with how fast it is going and what road it is on.

In the last chapter, I shared what I believe winning looks like and how I believe the church is doing: the church is losing. But I also shared what I believed about the church when I started in ministry—and I still believe it today. In short, I don't believe God's church can lose.

From my experience, I believe there are many reasons a team might lose. There are times when the other team is just better. But in this case we are talking about God's team, so I do not believe it is possible for God's team to lose. If we are losing, it is not because of how God designed the team.

HIS TEAM WINS!

In Matthew 16, Jesus tells Peter, "On this rock I will build my church, and the gates of Hades will not overcome it" (v. 18).

When I compare this statement with the church in America as a whole, I am left with a problem. Since I am a black-and-white kind of guy, I can only come up with two alternatives. Option 1:

Jesus is a liar because the gates of hell are prevailing against the church. Or option 2: The church that is being prevailed against isn't Jesus's church at all. Jesus did not promise the gates of hell would not prevail against *a* church but that it would not be able to stop *His* church.

Let's think through this for a minute; the statistics state that only about 2 to 5 percent (depending on the study) of churches are growing by conversion growth and 50 percent did not report a single convert last year, but Jesus said the gates of hell could not prevail against His church. The word for "prevail" also means prevent. In other words the gates of hell could not prevent the church from taking territory. In light of these facts, either Jesus was wrong or somehow the church in America has a problem.

WHERE DID WE GO WRONG?

As you look at the church over the centuries, you see one movement after another getting started with good hearts, only to fall into some kind of moral debauchery or doctrinal deviation. Many a group started well and lived for Jesus while the founders were alive, only to have someone later steer what they inherited in a different direction. Over and over leadership became about the rules, about a piece of land or a building, or about making everyone feel good regardless of their actions. The landscape is dotted with buildings that were built to hold an ever-growing congregation meant to glorify God, but they now stand empty.

How did this happen? Let's look at the Scripture for the warnings about most of the possible answers to this question.

TRAITS OF A LOSING TEAM

Paul frequently warned people not to allow the church to become anything other than Jesus's church. He says in 1 Corinthians 3:5, to those who would divide into camps based on personalities, "After all, who is Apollos? Who is Paul? We are only God's servants through whom you believed the Good News" (NLT). These people were forgetting that the church's purpose is to glorify God, not men. Over the years there have been many groups that became more enamored with their leader than they were with Jesus. No group that lives for the glory of a mere man can be blessed by God. The result: the team isn't God's team anymore.

Another example of a church gone wrong can be found just a few chapters later in 1 Corinthians 6:7. We find Paul blasting the church for bringing lawsuits against other believers. They had done this in front of unbelievers. He says to them, "The very fact that you have lawsuits among you means you have been completely defeated already." This passage reveals two truths. First, the Corinthian team cared more about their own individual rights than they did about the reputation of Jesus. They had forgotten that this world was not their home. They were adrift like everyone else in the world. They were lost in the sea of sin and purposelessness. So often churches forget their purpose, and when they do, no destination can be reached. As a result they are defeated. The team is losing because it isn't the Lord's team anymore.

Second, a team that fights with one another discredits the Prince of Peace, and no one will believe our message is based in truth. There are many evidences for Christianity, but the greatest is our testimony. We must not say one thing and do another. We were lost and alone, but now we have a growing relationship with God and others. The lonely world needs relationships like they need water. They are so thirsty for it. They must see we have it. When a church's leadership allows the flesh to rule unrestricted and unchecked, you can see the result, you can feel the strife. The church becomes a life-sucking entity instead of a life-giving body. A church that fights about personality issues, or non-salvation concerns, or the music, or the color of the carpet is defeated.

I believe God has no qualms about removing His blessing from a church that isn't being His church. He will allow the leadership's sinful natures to lead the church to where the sinful nature always leads us: death. It is better to have no church in an area than to have a church that makes Jesus look powerless and irrelevant.

A bad church is like an inoculation. To inoculate someone is to give them a small dose of a disease you don't want them to get. The body then develops antibodies so it can fight off the disease—the real thing. When people get a small dose of Christianity that doesn't accurately represent the real thing, then they think they know what the real thing is, but they actually don't. Many blame Jesus for what a "Christian" did to them. I know we all make mistakes and each one of us has given Jesus a black eye or two, but when that is the norm instead of the exception, people stop listening and the team loses.

Another reason a team might lose is found in 1 Corinthians 9:22–23. Paul makes it clear that he will do whatever it takes short of sin to reach the lost. He says it this way, "To the weak I became weak, to win the weak. I have become all things to all men so that by all possible means I might save some. I do all this for the sake of the gospel, that I may share in its blessings." So few are willing to step out of their comfort zone to see people come to know Jesus. Jesus became entirely uncomfortable to come and save us, but we want the lost to come to us on our terms. When we are not willing to work hard, to change, to step out to see people come to know Jesus, we have missed the heart of God. The team loses because we do not share the Lord's heart.

Yet another possibility for the losses may have something to do with our lack of seeing people as God sees them. At times I have heard people at Real Life complain about the smokers standing outside between services. I have also had people ask me why we allow hats to be worn in the house of the Lord. First, I remind them that the church building is not the house of the Lord. I point out that Christians are the temple of the Holy Spirit and the building we meet in is just a tool. Second, I remind them that Jesus came to seek and save the lost. Jesus would hang out with those the religious people would not dare be around. If our church does not have lost people hanging around, then I doubt Jesus is around either. Real Life welcomes those who don't necessarily look or always act like church people; we believe that is part of winning. And we believe Jesus thinks we are winning also.

There are many other reasons a team might fail, but let me just mention one more. Some of the coaches of God's teams have decided that they don't want to use the Lord's playbook, the Bible, anymore. They are more interested in hearing the praises of men, culture, politicians, etc., than they are the praises of God. They chase their tails trying to keep up with the culture. They put aside clear biblical teachings because they are unpopular; or they refuse to say sin is sin, and instead allow people to live as they want to, rather than how God directs. In this case God withdraws His blessing and the church loses.

STAYING DILIGENT

Let me close with this. We don't win every battle. We face an adversary who is crafty and relentless. He targets every winning church because he doesn't have to worry about losing churches—they are doing enough damage on their own. Every coach who is trying to turn around a losing church will have to be spiritually diligent. The devil hates us. He never stops coming. He distracts us, tempting us to settle down, or to not be so fanatical about winning. He says, "Don't aim so high. Chase an easier goal." He tries to discourage us with relational setbacks, with financial problems, or with health issues. Sometimes the enemy gets really sneaky and tries to get leaders to focus on working harder. Many pastors I have known do need to work harder; some act as though there is no hurry and there is nothing at stake. However, there are many others who work as hard as they can and still remain healthy and balanced. For those of us in that boat, the devil will try to get us too busy to stop and pray, to take vacation, or to pastor our most important sheep—our family.

Often my balance is tenuous and I can be inclined to miss my times with the Lord. When that happens, I start functioning on my own wisdom, strength, and experience. I think to myself, *I have dealt with this before and I know what to do.* I forget that every situation is different and I need the Lord to give me discernment.

I know to pray when I am fighting a huge monster I have never fought before. But it's the times I am dealing with things I have knowledge about that I forget to seek the Lord. The more I work on the lists in my head in my own strength, the more work I make for myself. The more of Jim's wisdom I use, the more I get what only I can get, and usually it is trouble.

Sometimes it gets discouraging. It seems that we lose so many battles. I have to remind myself that God has promised that we will not lose the war if we are on His team. He has promised us that He will help us to win the way He sees winning. He will help us reach people, disciple them, and send them to do the same. If that is not happening on your team, then there is a problem. Somehow the team has lost its purpose.

God often wakes me up with a slap across the face. There are times I suffer from vision drift, get distracted or discouraged. It may be painful or frustrating, but He demonstrates His love when He brings someone to me to ask tough questions or has me read something that challenges me or causes me to question my motives. He loves His church so much that He will discipline us to refocus and ask again, "What in the world am I doing?"

Are you open to God's leading? Is He your Head coach? Are you using His playbook? Is He being glorified in your life and the life of your church?

05

WINNING STARTS AT THE TOP

The Need for Coaches in the Church

Every owner of a professional sports team knows his team can have the greatest players and still lose. Everyone from high school athletic directors to pro sports teams are looking for coaches who can lead their teams to victory. Even those who have little understanding of sports have experienced the effects a bad coach can have on an individual player or on a team as a whole.

Many of us have suffered the agony of watching our children play Little League baseball or youth soccer for coaches who did not understand the game well enough to win. As parents, if the team wins, we honor the hard work of the coach. If we lose, we place at least part of the blame on the coach. Competent coaches are imperative to a winning team.

A coach is expected to lead. It is part of the job. We do not pay for our kids to play in a sport where there is little control and leadership. We don't want our kids to dictate the pace or the schedule—we want them to learn, to improve. Yes, we want them to enjoy themselves, but that seldom happens for the team that continues to lose.

The church needs a good coach as well. Many a search committee looks for the right pastor to lead their church. They expect the pastor to lead the church to victory, and if that doesn't happen, they look for another pastor.

In wrestling (truly a biblical sport; see Gen. 32:24), we have a saying: "If you kill the head, the body dies." It's harsh, but true. The objective of a wrestler is to attack the head of the opponent. If you can disable the brain, the body can't defend itself and it can't attack. In the same way, if the head (local leadership) of the church is dysfunctional, the body can't function as it should, and it leads to a losing season. Winning starts with good leadership, on the field and in the church.

PLAYER OR COACH?

When I was a player, I had a player's mind-set. I wanted to compete at the highest level, so I concentrated on acquiring and honing the skills and stamina that I would need to win on the mat or field. My focus was on my position, and I hoped everyone else would carry their own weight. If each part of the team did their job, we would win.

When I became a coach, my job was no longer about what position I was going to play; I was no longer going to play a position. My job was to develop people so that they could play their positions or wrestle their weights. It was no longer about what I would do on the mat or field. It was about what I could train the athletes to do in their moment of decision.

There is nothing worse than having a player in a coach's position. For my senior year of college, I transferred to a school where one of the great American wrestlers had recently joined the coaching staff. I thought being coached by him would help me get to the next level. However, I soon discovered that he was not there to coach me; instead, I was there to help him train for the Olympics.

When I would beat him in practice, he would become angry and tell me I was just lucky. He would say in a condescending tone that there is no way he should lose a point to someone like me. Rather than seeing an opportunity to build me up and give me the confidence I would need to win, he would be frustrated at my progress or his lack thereof. That year, I learned that sometimes a coach doesn't understand what it means to be a coach; that a person may still consider himself a player, which in turn produces a skewed mind-set. When that happens, it is detrimental to the people he is supposed to mold.

WHAT IS A COACH?

Just as a coach can hurt the team by not understanding his role, a pastor can hurt the church for the same reason. God has given His coaches a job description in Ephesians 4:11–13:

> It was he [Jesus] who gave some to be apostles, some to be prophets, some to be evangelists, and some to be pastors and teachers, *to prepare God's people for works of service*, so that the body of Christ may be built up *until we all reach unity in the faith and in the knowledge of the Son of God and become mature, attaining to the whole measure of the fullness of Christ* (emphasis added).

This passage tells us that the job of a pastor has two parts. First, they are to prepare or equip God's players to play, or in biblical terminology, to serve one another and reach out to the world. Secondly, pastors are to lead their people to become unified. No team, no matter how great the players, can win if they are not unified. The team must have the same goal, the same language; they must have a common understanding of the part they play; and they must work together to achieve that goal.

The "Big Four" mentality permeates our churches. Pastors are taught that if they have (1) good preaching, (2) good worship, (3) good children's ministries, and (4) good location, they will have a big church. Remember, the goal for many is numbers; numbers mean they are winning, so they seek to gather a crowd. The churches that put on a good show for everyone will get the biggest crowds. Their success depends on having good children's and youth shows as well.

Don't get me wrong. I do not have a problem with being good at any of these things. In fact, I think that they are imperative to success. They are the front door to so much more. I also don't have a problem with *big*. A healthy church grows. At Real Life we want to reach every person in our area; we want to grow, so we plan new ways to do so. But again, just because a church is big doesn't mean it's healthy.

As a result of a pastor's "show" mentality, many Christians have come to believe their job is to attend the show. According to statistics, most Christians attend church 1.6 times a month. Few are involved in any kind of a small group or Bible study, or serve in their community or church. In other words, they go to church on Sunday because they think that is all that they are expected to do. In reality, it is all they are trained to do.

The Scriptures tell us that we are to be part of a team that works together to achieve God's purposes. We don't go to church; we *are* the church. In a church you are invited to volunteer; on a team you are *expected* to play a part.

A coach's job is to make sure everyone understands his obligation to the team. A coach makes sure every player understands what "the Owner" requires. The One who bought us for a price expects us to play. Winning is not gathering a crowd. It's raising, training, and releasing a team.

THE PAID-PLAYER MENTALITY

Let me point out again that somehow pastors have come to believe that they are the paid players, and the people who attend are the fans. Game day is Sunday and the building is the arena. People in the area will follow the best team in town, so ours better be the best. The elders or board members are the general managers and owners who watch to make sure the people are getting what they pay for. They make business decisions that ensure the team can win for years to come. The money (offering) that goes into the bucket is the admission price.

We don't want to offend our best box seat owners so we say little that will upset anyone. We want them to have a *good experience*, which is usually defined by telling people what they want to hear. So we say things like, "God wants to make you rich," "God wants to make you healthy," and "God wants you to be happy," hoping that people will flock to our church.

When senior pastors buy into the star-player approach, they believe the key to gathering a bigger crowd is tied to their own preaching performance. If they could play better, more would come to watch them play. The result is that they expend most of their energy trying to teach something new, or say something old in a newer and better way. It's easy to see how this can happen. People become enamored with a speaker's personal charisma. He can really wow the masses, so more come to watch him play. He may write several books that put him in high demand across America. He can even come to believe that the team exists to make him look good. It may feed his ego and in doing so create a monster. We men especially have a need to achieve, and success breeds ego.

When the paid-player mentality guides the church, everything becomes a show, and soon they think they have to have a whole cast of paid professionals to create little spectacles for their assigned demographic groups. So the answer is to pay big money for franchise players who will give a great performance that will draw the thousands of kids and youth in their area. They scour the land to steal a great player from another team, while their best players are being scouted as well.

Most of the money given by the fans is used for the development of a better show, not for helping people or building new players. Because the show is so important, they spend most of the week developing the next show and have little time for relationship with the people in the church. They send the counseling appointments to an agency while they spend forty hours a week trying to find a new way to wow the crowd. They are always compelled to try something that has never been done, or to try what other big churches are doing, or to try to mimic what people are seeing in Hollywood—all the while forgetting that the Spirit of God, not the show, is what really changes people.

THE POWER OF RELATIONSHIPS

As Real Life grew, we came to a real crossroads. Our small band of leaders and I believed in shepherding our people. We believed in relationship, in real discipleship, but we had grown past our ability to do that successfully in the way we had in the past. Really, the problem was mine. At that point I did much of the work without seeking help. I had fallen into another hazard of the paid-player mentality. I had started to think it was my job to carry the team. I had taken too much responsibility. I had forgotten that a team can only win as a team. It wasn't about creating a great show so much as falling into the trap of believing it was my job to take care of all the sheep. It was killing me and I was losing my joy, in spite of the fact that we were in the middle of a miracle. It was also stalling our growth, as I was no longer able to care for all the people as I once had.

I had never been in a church this size. We looked around at bigger churches to see how they handled these challenges. Our questions were: How do you pastor the masses in your church? How do you call the missing, counsel the hurting, and train people for ministry? How do you maintain a relationship-based team that loves one another and at the same time put together a meaningful service for Sunday morning?

Most of the churches that we sought council from had come to the same crossroads and had decided to focus on the show. It was obvious because they were spending their time and money dealing with things pertaining to the show. I am not saying their hearts were bad. I just believe that somehow many pastors have forgotten what is truly important.

We had choices of our own to make. We could become an entertainment center and put on a show too. After all, maybe they were right. Maybe it wasn't reasonable to try to pastor that many people. But we believed that the miracle we were witnessing was happening because we had not strayed from the simple commands found in the Scriptures, and because we had tried our best, whether or not we always succeeded. Besides, we were like many churches in the country. We couldn't afford the stuff it took to put on that kind of production, even if we wanted to. Even if someone had given it to us, we did not have the staff who would know how to run it.

At that point we realized that we had started down a path we did not believe in and could not continue. We realized how easy it is to slide into the "show" mentality. It starts subtly. The more the church grows numerically, the harder it becomes to hold to your values, and what is expedient can come naturally. It's easy to talk yourself into believing that it is your job to put on a good show, and it is the people's job to come.

It is easy because it is almost true. The enemy loves to tell us things that are almost true. Yes, it is the people's job to be committed and to make the Lord's work a priority. But it is the shepherd's job to chase the strays. If after we have chased them, they refuse to come home, then they are at fault. As I look at many pastors, I don't see many chasers anymore. People have become numbers to be counted rather than souls to be cared for.

The show mentality can be dangerous for many reasons. For example, there is very little loyalty when it comes to a movie theatre in your area. You will go to the one with the best price, the best sound system, the one closest to your home, or the one with the movie you want to see. If you rely on a show to keep your people, it better be good! People get bored quickly and they are extremely fickle. If you got them because your show is the best in town, they will leave when they find a better one.

Conversely, if you love your people and help them grow in their relationship with Jesus and find relationships with others on your team, people will put up with less because *they know they are loved*. If people know they are loved, and have been affected by your mission, they will be more likely to get involved in it. Their commitment level grows and will hold them to the Lord's church that you lead.

I have found that knowing and loving your people answers the question of how to build a meaningful worship experience as well. If you *know your people*, you will know what they are dealing with. You will have spent time getting to know how they parent, how they work, what they care about, where they are in their relationship with God. You will then naturally shape your messages toward what they need, rather than stealing sermons from a big church in a different city. Your people will feel as if you are talking straight to them. You will hear comments like, "Were you a fly on my wall last night?" You will reach people where they live, allowing the Word to challenge them.

If your church is relational, your people will enjoy being together. They will want to come to see their friends. If you pastor people, they will come because they know they will get help when they are struggling. If this pastoral, relational environment is created by everyone on your staff, the worship experience will be meaningful to all. They will look up at your worship leader and think, *That guy loves Jesus and he loves me.* They will see a genuine fellow traveler on the stage, and they will relate. As far as I am concerned, I would rather have a man who leads from the heart and truly desires to direct the attention to Jesus, than a master of music who can only wow the crowd with his amazing musical ability. The result of the first guy's work will be people drawn into worship that extends past the singing.

DITCHING THE SHOW MENTALITY

God's idea of a coach is one who creates a system that develops people into great players. It is true that we have a part to play on

Sunday mornings. We do try to motivate and teach as best we can the masses of people who come to our services. However, a good coach develops a way to turn those he gathers and leads into great players. He creates a way to guide them into their position on the team. Every person is a player. Success is creating a team that can work together. Success is finding and developing players who will later become coaches themselves.

When I look at churches filled with people who have come to watch the show and I don't see any intentional attempt to move people into the discipleship process, it saddens me. A congregation that is informed about the game is not the same as a congregation that is committed to learning how to play the game.

Jesus didn't work that way. He knew many in the crowd only wanted a show, a meal, a healing. They came to receive without giving, without commitment. Jesus knew that, to change the world, He needed to focus on sold-out disciples. He had to take these men through a shaping process that would leave them looking like Himself. There was a place for the crowds—He preached there, He healed there. But His intention was to pour Himself into those who would take up their crosses and follow Him. His method worked. The world heard about God's saving grace because He developed fishers of men.

In the next chapters, we will further define the work of a coach. We will explore how a coach does his two jobs of building great players and getting great players to play together.

Before we take that next step, let me ask you some important questions. In fact, if you get nothing else out of this book, I hope these questions are the ones you'll spend the most effort on:

How much of your time is spent on the show?
How much of your staff's time is spent working on the next game day—Sunday?
Do you believe that all the people in your church are potential players? Are you pouring yourself into them?
Are you developing a team culture?

Are you motivating your people to come to the next show, or are you showing them how to be used on the team?

By the way you lead, are you creating an army or a nursery? An army conquers the enemy and takes their territory. A nursery feeds the children, wipes their fannies, and tries to get them to stop whining and crying.

What kind of a team are you creating?

A Coach Worth Following

Discovering Our God-Given Purpose

So the goal of a coach is to follow God's guidance toward creating a team that can win. A *winning* team is one that reaches the lost and makes disciples who can disciple others. The goal of winning is not to fill stadiums with fans; it's not about numbers, unless what you are counting is the number of godly disciples. Life change is the goal.

Winning with Heart

Sometimes coaches understand how to play the game and how to discern who best fits where. They are able to see holes in the opposition and they have a brilliant mind, but they may still miss something very important.

The greatest coach I ever had was special, not just because he understood wrestling, but because he understood people. He cared very much about winning and he worked hard to achieve it, but unlike many leaders, people never became objects to maneuver for his own success. This coach cared about me as a person. There were times when I could not help the team win, but he proved over and over that he still cared about me. You find out what a person values by how he treats people who can't add value to the person's reputation or success.

I had always wanted to win, but when I wrestled on his team I didn't want to win just for me. I wanted to win for him. He believed in me and cared for me, so I listened when he spoke. I tried harder just because he had inspired me, not with a great speech, but with his actions when I wasn't wrestling or when I was losing. It not only motivated me to try harder, but it shaped the way I would later coach.

Great coaches have something special that many knowledgeable leaders lack. The Bible uses a word that I think describes a great coach perfectly—*shepherd*.

God Expects His Leaders to Shepherd

Coaching is more than just informing others *about* the game we play. Often when we share Christ with someone and they make a decision, we put a notch on our Bible and head off to share Christ with others. What that new believer doesn't understand, and what we don't tell them, is that they are only *starting* a race, not *finishing* one. We are addicted to what we think is a win. Our cheer: "Oh yeah, I got another one!" We say, "It's my job to tell them and God's job to clean them up."

We forget that the devil now sees the one we just baptized as an *enemy*. This is not like a physical game we might play, where at worst we get hurt accidentally and need medical attention. Satan is not happy about losing that person to Jesus. Depending on your theology, some believe Satan will attempt to get the new believer back; others believe he will endeavor to make them useless to the Lord's cause. Either way, he is out to disarm and destroy them to protect his own evil kingdom.

We often don't understand that we just got this new believer into a war they are not equipped to fight. They don't know the rules, or the weapons available, or even how to use them. Those we win to Christ need someone to develop and nurture them. They start the game with little ability to help the team win, but they are still very important to God and His church. They have great potential.

Every player needs to go through a process of learning that will eventually lead him or her to become fully equipped to play the game. The coach's job is to guide the rookie by creating a climate of shepherding. We teach them and allow them to make mistakes. We must disciple our people. It starts with taking responsibility not just for winning the lost but for shepherding them too. The pastor can't do this by himself. Part of his job is to create a shepherding environment where everyone is challenged to shepherd others and win the lost.

This became clear to me several years ago when we first started Real Life Ministries. I met a young man at a wrestling tournament who was in trouble and on the verge of losing his family. I invited him to a men's breakfast/Bible study where we were going through a passage of Scripture that revealed there is a cost to discipleship. I was explaining that Jesus had called us to abandon our stuff and follow Him and that He calls us to be in a discipleship relationship with Him and others. As the conversation continued, I could see something was troubling this young man, so I asked him to tell us what he was thinking.

He explained that his marriage was in trouble, and he didn't know what to do. He said something I will never forget. "I went to a church event in another state two years ago, and I knew I was in trouble then. The preacher spoke of grace and strength that comes from starting a relationship with Jesus. I gave my life to the Lord and prayed with the man who was waiting at the front of the church. He gave me some material and invited me to church the following week. I decided I wanted to quit drugs, pornography . . . everything, but I didn't know how. I didn't know the Word. I didn't have any relationships with believers."

He continued. "I started to attend church. I even went to the men's breakfast, but I had questions. I tried to make an appointment with *anyone* who looked like they knew what they were talking about, but they were too busy. I knew my friends were headed down destructive paths, so I tried to start new relationships at church, but no one would return my phone calls. When they did, they were too busy to meet."

As he spoke, emotion welled up within him. He was a huge man who had been a football player in college, yet he stood before this group of men on the verge of breaking down. He said, "You don't need to tell new believers that they need to be discipled or that they need new relationships. We know. I think you should talk to these Christian leaders about being too busy for us. What's the point of telling us to follow if you are not going to show us how?"

THE RESPONSIBILITY THAT COMES WITH THE JOB

Many of us like gathering a crowd because we get a sense that we are successful when many seek our advice and tell us we are great. We feel important, needed, smart, and in some cases, powerful and influential. Many of us like the spotlight but do not want the responsibility that comes with it.

Jesus gave us the example of a true shepherd when He gave up His life for us. In Acts 20:28, Paul tells the elders to shepherd the flock of which he had made them overseers. He reminds the leaders in that passage that the sheep were purchased by God. In other words, we have a responsibility given by God to watch His sheep, so we must do it well. In James 3:1 we are warned to be careful about assuming a role of leadership, because we will be given a stricter judgment. I don't believe for a minute that God doesn't want many leaders, many who can train up others. I believe this warning is intended to warn potential leaders that this role cannot be for personal glory. There are responsibilities attached.

God describes His expectations of a shepherd in Ezekiel 34:2–10:

> This is what the Sovereign LORD says: Woe to the shepherds of Israel who only take care of themselves! Should not shepherds take care of the flock? You eat the curds, clothe yourselves with the wool and slaughter the choice animals, but you do not take care of the flock. . . . You have not brought back the strays or searched for the lost. . . . So they were scattered because there was no shepherd. . . .
>
> Therefore, you shepherds, hear the word of the LORD: As surely as I live, declares the Sovereign LORD, because my flock lacks a shepherd and so has been plundered and has become food for all the wild animals, and because my shepherds did not search for my flock but cared for themselves rather than for my flock . . . I am against the shepherds and will hold them accountable for my flock. I will remove them from tending the flock so that the shepherds can no longer feed themselves.

We see God judging the shepherds because they failed to fulfill their responsibility—they had not fed the sheep but only themselves. Many leaders in the world today lead in order to feed their own ego. This is not an option for God's shepherds. A shepherd must care for the needs of the sheep for their good and because the shepherd wants to obey the Lord.

In Ezekiel 34, the sheep were not cared for. When they were hurt, they were not nursed back to health. When they strayed or were lost, the shepherd didn't look for them. They became food for wild animals. This is what happens in the church when God's people are not shepherded.

Notice how God defines the role of a spiritual leader. He wants a shepherd to care for the people placed under him: God's sheep. Unfortunately, sheep stink, bite, and wander, and they can be stubborn. Yet God expects shepherds to care for His flock. They are to tend to the wounds of His sheep and rein in those who stray if possible. It's for their own good but some will fight against it.

For leaders who call themselves pastors but determine their success by how many attend church, my question to them is, "How do you define the word *pastor*?" If the response is, "A pastor is one who teaches people about God," I disagree. A teacher teaches and a pastor shepherds. Both are offices in the church, and both jobs are essential to the success of God's team. However, those who call themselves pastors but only attempt to transfer information are not pastors. Teachers transfer information. Yes, teachers should also care about their sheep, but it is the pastors who are to make sure the shepherding is getting done.

Many pastors teach but are not around when the sheep need help. Granted, a pastor can't do everything, but his responsibility is to make sure all the positions on the team are filled. Every one of the offices in Ephesians 4 is important. God gave some to be apostles, prophets, evangelists, pastors, and teachers. Each of these positions when filled will lead to a healthy team (church).

Every coach needs to have a game plan for shepherding the hurting and chasing strays. We are often like the hired hand Jesus talks about. When the wolf comes, we run or ignore the plight of the sheep because we don't really love them. One of the most disturbing experiences I have with pastors is when I explain how we try to call all the missing, even in a church of thousands. The comments range from "How can you possibly do that?" to "Why would you want to do that?" To the first group, we explain that it is our job to figure out how, no matter how hard it is. To the second group, we respond, "Why wouldn't you want to check on your people? Don't take the job if you are not going to try to complete the assignments given by the Owner of the sheep."

The sad thing is that I often hear pastors rail against the secular world counselors because they teach our people unbiblical things. But we don't give them any alternatives. Many pastors are so busy preparing for the next show that they cannot shepherd their sheep. I know a pastor can do only so much, but we have an obligation to guide our people toward Jesus when they are in trouble. We do not do it because we are paid. We do it because we can't do anything else. We love God and we love His people, so we help them understand the Word. We help them understand God's will for their lives. We also help them understand how God created them and equipped them for service. We help them understand church life and work life and help them find a small group family where their needs can be met.

Sometimes, shepherding means getting dirty. People's lives are messy, and it takes time for the Lord to clean them up. Too often our lives are so busy that the only people we can see ourselves working with are those who won't take much time. We don't think in terms of relationship; we think in terms of information. We hand people a book, send them to a great class, or give them a CD, but we don't spend the time it takes to walk with them. The right question is not "How do I find time for that in my busy schedule?" The right question is "How do I change my life so I can do what the Lord requires of me as a leader?"

SHEPHERDING EARNS YOU THE RIGHT TO LEAD

One of our pastors, Dan Lynch, is a biblical archaeologist. He has been to Israel numerous times. He tells a story that is a magnificent illustration of a good shepherd.

> One time I was walking just outside of Jerusalem, when I came upon a valley with a watering hole at the bottom. At the watering hole, I watched a flock of sheep with many shepherds. As I watched, one shepherd walked to the top of the hill and whistled. I then realized this was not one flock with many shepherds but many flocks with shepherds for each flock. The shepherd who whistled never looked back. As he walked, his sheep that had intermingled with all the other flocks were now starting to separate and follow their shepherd up the hill. They weren't being driven, they just followed on their own. A good shepherd does not drive sheep; he leads them and they follow.

Volunteer organizations are unique. People do not have to follow. You can't hold a paycheck over their head. You don't have the power to make them do anything. If you want to lead a volunteer organization, you have to understand people will only follow if they want to. They will only follow if they believe you care for them. I'm sure we have all had someone try to lead us before we had any kind of relationship with them. We wonder, *Who do you think you are?* We begin to trust a leader only after he has proven himself to us through right decision making and only when we sense his love for us. It takes patience, time, risk, and heart to lead sheep!

As a coach and a shepherd of Real Life, I cannot *pastor* 8,000 people. My responsibility is to follow the Lord's plan for creating a shepherding culture and community. I must raise up those who help me accomplish the objective given to us by the Lord. If you think you are a shepherd, but no one is following you, then it's time to *earn the right* to be followed by shepherding God's way.

Most of us think this means writing better sermons, but you have heard the true statement that "people don't care how much you know until they know how much you care." A leader must be someone who knows his sheep and understands their needs. He leads them, teaches them, and models for them how to serve God and others. There is mutual accountability and trust. The shepherd knows when his sheep have succeeded, and he celebrates with them. He knows when they feel defeated and need encouragement and support. He grieves with them, and when the sheep wander, he does all he can to get them back on track.

THE RESULT OF A SHEPHERDING CULTURE

A shepherding church grows. It can't help it. There has never been a faster growing church than the one in Acts. Paul could say that the whole world had heard about Jesus within sixty years of the church's beginning, even though they didn't have access to the Internet, television, or radio. The best way to reach your community is often simple.

Remember the sheep intermingled with other flocks at the watering hole? As Dan told me that story, I was blown away by his statement: "A good shepherd does not drive sheep; he leads them and they follow." Jesus said the same thing in John 10:27: "My sheep listen to my voice; I know them, and they follow me."

Here's a parable for you to ponder. Imagine that sheep are smart enough to speak to one another. One day several flocks of sheep had been led by their shepherds to one large, central watering hole. As they were mingling and wandering about, one rather disheveled-looking sheep notices another sheep from a different flock. He sees that his wool is clean, white as snow. This is truly unusual in the flock that the dirty sheep comes from. Everyone in his flock is messed up, with sores in their eyes and ticks on their skin. The dirty sheep sighs deeply, and says to the clean sheep, "Wow, you look so clean and healthy! Your shepherd must really care about you."

The well-groomed sheep says, "Oh yes! My shepherd loves me. Every day he picks the burrs from my wool, oils my eyes, strokes my head, and whispers in my ear that he loves me."

As the mangy sheep listens, he takes a hard look at himself and thinks, "My shepherd doesn't seem to care about me at all. He has never even touched me."

The well-groomed sheep testifies, "My shepherd has fought great battles with wild animals to save me and my fellow sheep. One time he even put us in a safe place and left us to find a lamb that had wandered away."

About that time, the shepherd of the well-groomed sheep gives a call. All those that belong to him take off with a jolt. He does not need to plead with them; they follow him because they love him. They trust the shepherd.

The shepherd walks ahead; he doesn't need to look back because he knows his sheep will follow. As he reaches the crest of the hill, something strange happens. He hears shouts. Turning around, he sees more sheep than he anticipated. Most of the sheep in the valley are right behind him, and the shepherds of those sheep are chasing them up the hill.

As the sheep of the other shepherds mingle among the good shepherd's sheep, they begin to compare themselves to the well-cared-for sheep. They ask, "What makes you different?" It doesn't take many testimonies to convince them they want to follow a new shepherd.

There are many applications in this parable. Of course, the first would be that Jesus is the Good Shepherd. He cleans us and cares for us. We all follow something—a philosophy, a leader, a teacher—and we become like that which we chase. If we follow a wrestler, our ears will eventually look funny, our necks will get larger, and our noses flatter. If we follow a rock band, we will look like the lead guitarist, the drummer, or the bass player. Those of us who follow Jesus look different. When we look like Jesus, those in the world will notice, and many will say, "I want a new way of life. I want a new shepherd. I have followed another and have been hurt. I have been the shepherd of my own heart, and it hasn't worked out. I will follow you and your shepherd."

There is another application to this story that applies to pastors and churches. One of the things I have heard around town about our church is that we *steal* sheep. This statement drives me crazy. Yes, we have had people come from other fellowships even though many of our people are new converts. Some will leave Real Life too. There are also those who won't really be happy anywhere. For these folks, the problem isn't the place; it is within themselves. However, some leave the flock they used to be a part of because they had no shepherd. There was no one to care for them, develop them, and release them. Sometimes if a sheep is "stolen," it is the fault of the shepherd.

In a church world that is often more interested in a show or a façade, one of the benefits of taking care of your sheep is that the saved and the unsaved will follow your sheep home. Some feel that if people come from another flock, they should be sent home. It is not my place to choose for people where they attend church. However, I can say that sheep need to be cared for. People need to grow, to be loved, and to be developed. I would never send people back to a place that does not care about their well-being or growth.

We all know that word of mouth is the best way to reach a community. The Internet, newspaper, mailers, and phone calls just don't work as well. When people get excited about something, they share it with those they know. When someone comes to know Jesus, they get excited about this newfound purpose, and they share it! Discipleship begins with who they know.

WALKING BILLBOARDS FOR JESUS

In every church, there is an army waiting to be released. They work in almost every place of business, and if they could be empowered, trained, and released, they would change the world with their actions and their voices. At first, people they share with might take a "we'll see" attitude, and sometimes they will take an anti-Christian stance, but when they see someone really change, it draws them closer.

When a church becomes a shepherding community, when they care for the needs of others, when they help people beat the habits that have always beaten *them*, when they dare to be real, others can't help but notice. They see joy and a change in the person they have always known, and they become interested—even excited. At the very least, they keep watching. This has been how our church has grown—through the Holy Spirit changing people's lives.

When a shepherding culture goes the extra mile, people get involved in others' lives and become a community. When they see the power of God in those they love, they are drawn. It's contagious! People literally become walking billboards for Jesus. In a world of brokenness, what a relief to find real relationships, real family, and real help.

God's coaches get the best out of their players. Yes, they teach them how to play and how to play well together, but how do they do it? They show their people that they love them. They earn the right to lead. They create a culture of love by modeling it. That is a coach worth following, a coach who looks a lot like Jesus.

PART 3

DEVELOPING
SKILLED PLAYERS

GOOD RECRUITING

Outreach Events, Programs, and Weekend Services

Churches often have stated goals but behaviors that circumvent or work against them. For instance, we might say we want to reach the world, but we do things that keep us from being in contact with the world we want to reach. We plan an outreach, but it is really designed to attract people who already think like us (other believers). We don't know how to relate to lost folks, so we pray and expect that God will bring them to us. The Scriptures tell us that we are to "go into the world," that the gates of hell cannot prevail against us. What we don't seem to understand is that this Scripture means the gates of hell cannot prevent us from winning. The goal of a church is to reach out—to share our faith. All of us are to share our faith as individuals, but we can also do things corporately that we cannot do alone.

REACHING OUT WITH BRIDGES

At Real Life we do a variety of special outreach events. We call them bridges. They are designed to meet unsaved people in a place that will allow them to be comfortable. Two of our largest events are our community Easter Egg Hunt and our Harvest Festival held on Halloween night. We try to utilize times that people would normally look for a community activity and give them alternatives that could ultimately bridge them to the church body. Our team strives to make sure that everything we do has a purpose. If we are to create a successful event, we must first identify the perceived needs of those we wish to attract. We then have "bait" that attracts them. After all, we are fishers of men (Matt. 4:19). We must create an environment that fulfills the purpose of the combined effort of our team. If we say we want to reach non-Christians, but we choose an event that only Christians would attend, we have failed. We may steal Christians from other churches but not see anyone saved. This would mean that we did not succeed.

A good outreach event always bridges people to the next step in the process. We know the goal is to see them become disciples who can disciple others. Our goal at the outreach event is to make sure they are invited into the next step in the process. We must have a process in place to take them to that next step.

Let's use the example of an elk-calling seminar sponsored by our Sports and Outdoors Ministry. We ask men and women in our church to invite their non-Christian friends who are interested in hunting to a dinner. We also advertise the event in all the hunting stores in the area. At the dinner we have a speaker who is well known in his hunting specialty. This famous hunter is a Christian, who shares hunting tips and then gives his testimony. At the end of the event we invite the men to come to the monthly men's breakfast. From there they are invited to a small group that meets weekly for breakfast in a local restaurant. In our church every road eventually leads to a small group where real discipleship can happen.

At all of these meetings men are invited to start a relationship with Jesus and to come to church on the weekend. Because of the connections that happen at each event, a man who would not have thought of attending church now has friends there waiting for him.

THE PURPOSE OF A CHURCH SERVICE

Some might think that since I have written against a "show" mentality in a church that I am advocating getting rid of the weekend worship service. On the contrary, I believe they are very important. Our services are designed not only to encourage those who are already Christians but to receive those who were attracted through our bridge events. I do not want to imply that we shouldn't do a good job with weekend worship services. I do care that the sermon is well written, the choir or worship team can sing, and the worship is meaningful. My definition of excellence is to do the best you possibly can, so I want our services to be awesome! After all, the worship service can lead to the rest of what we do.

In our American culture, the first place a person might come if they are looking for a church is to a service. This is especially true when the churched move into an area. It may also be true for those who were brought up in a church but left it for one reason or another. Even non-Christians will attend a service if they are investigating the claims of the Bible. Therefore, we want our service to be an experience they will want to try again.

I believe there is a real purpose for a worship service. Some leaders have decided to abandon the church service altogether, while others have made it the all-important component of what they do. But a well-designed worship experience can be a great way to bridge someone from the world to a relational environment for discipleship (small groups). I believe it is possible to cause both the saved and the unsaved to want more of God by creating an effective worship experience.

For the churched, the worship service is an opportunity to create an environment that edifies the Christian through worship, ministry, some teaching, and some fellowship (real fellowship cannot happen during an hour-and-a-half service). Ultimately, Sunday should be the locker room talk before a team hits the field. It's the "Go get 'em!" speech that says, "Remember, here is the game plan. Now let's go do it!" It rallies the team to get them wholeheartedly into each part of the needed process. It reminds them to get back out there and win!

Sunday is not the best time to teach deep theological truths, however. Most people have short attention spans and don't retain knowledge through the lecture method. Americans are used to a visual culture, and those who do attend church are gauging a service's success by their personal boredom meter. Don't try to do too much. Your main goal is to inspire people to go to the next step.

For the unchurched people who attend our church, we want them to say, "Hey, this wasn't like what I thought it would be like. The people were cool, friendly, but not in your face. They were dressed normal, not at all stuffy. The music was good, not some tune from the early 1800s. I could actually understand the speaker; he didn't use big words. He didn't expect me to know things I don't know. He explained why they believe the way they do and how it applies to me. He told his people to live out the lifestyle of love. He told them to be real. My kids had a good time and were cared for. Man! They even have good coffee!"

We want to surprise the unchurched. They have a picture in their minds of what Christians look like and how they act. I know that picture too well; it was my picture for many years, and it kept me out of the church. I want to change that picture.

We want Christianity to make sense and reflect genuine love. If we reflect Jesus, if we show people His heart and His wisdom, the unchurched may be drawn to church. I am absolutely sure it works because I see it every week. I want the church building and service to be places where neither the churched nor the unchurched would be embarrassed to bring their friends. Remember the church grows by word of mouth. No one will bring people to something that will embarrass them.

THINKING STRATEGICALLY
ABOUT A WORSHIP SERVICE

To create an effective environment, you have to break down every part of what you do and ask some important questions: Is this biblical? Will this move someone to where we want to take them next? Is this as relational as we can make it? Is this relevant and applicable to life? The answers to these questions depend on your target audience.

At Real Life we have decided that we want to attract the person who is finished with religion and is ready for an authentic relationship with God and others. Religious people will feel very uncomfortable with what we do, but that is okay, because they are not our target. We define religious people as those who think that by following the rules, being good enough, righteous-looking enough, they are justified. They tend to be judgmental and like to fight. It is not that we don't want religious people, because we believe anyone can be changed, but reaching religious people is not our primary goal.

Secondly, we are targeting men. This is not to be exclusive, as we want everyone to come to know Christ. We have ministries and small groups geared toward everyone in our church. However, statistics tell us that if you can draw the man in the home to church, you have a better chance of bringing in the whole family. We think this is the best way to show love to women too. That might sound strange at first, but how many wives do you know who would do almost anything to have their husbands or sons want to come to church? We want men to be drawn into the service because they understand what is happening. They relate to the language and the style of teaching. They see men of all kinds taking part in what is happening. I love it when I look out on the crowd and see big, tough men with tears on their faces. I love to see men leading their families to church. I love to see men hugging other men with big strong hugs. We want men to see that church is a place for them. We especially want to challenge them to be all that God wants them to be.

As leaders we often ask ourselves the question, "What are we doing with our services that appeals to men and would make them want to invite their friends?" For example, men love action—and the Bible is full of it. Men also tend to shy away from a lot of emotion, so worship style can quickly affect their comfort level.

MUSIC

When it comes to music, look to the Word to decide what part music is to play in a service. Worship at Real Life is about us getting out of the way and allowing our people to spend time with the Lord. We want our music to be good, but the focus needs to be on how good our God is, not on how good our musicians and singers are. For the unchurched, we want them to say, "Whoa! That was good, but something made it special."

People need to feel comfortable to stand and close their eyes if need be. They should not be made to feel guilty if they don't sing at the top of their lungs. As they grow, they may make the transition to express themselves in public worship. However, public displays of emotion can be something many shy away from because of their upbringing, so lighting matters. I believe the darker the better, because it makes people feel alone with God. The more they are made to feel like they are the only ones there, the more they may worship publicly. The less they can hear themselves, the more they may sing. The longer the singing time, the more uncomfortable many may feel, especially those who are unfamiliar with why we sing. We are trying to bridge lost people into an entirely new culture.

God inhabits the praises of His people. So when they are worshiping, God shows up—He is there, and they feel God's presence. If our people are not worshiping, we've failed.

To worship does not mean everyone must be singing. I don't know when singing became synonymous with worship, but it is not the only means of worship. I have seen people weeping and others looking down quietly in thought. I'm okay with that. We succeeded if God and man are doing business together.

THE SERMON

Every Sunday service includes a message. This is not a time to inundate people with as much Bible knowledge as we can cram into a half-hour or forty-five-minute lecture (see chapter 9). It has to be well planned, well prepared, and well executed with the right intentions. Preaching has the potential to impact both the churched and the unchurched. We do not need to dumb down our preaching to target the unchurched. We can and have to teach biblical truth. However, we must make allowances for the unchurched or they will not desire to hear more. For that matter, the churched usually don't understand the Word either. So we can't assume either group knows who Abraham was or what the correct meaning of *sanctification* is. We need to use words people understand and give enough of the story so everyone understands the point. In fact, the more you use stories, the better the learning. We live in a culture of stories, and the Bible is full of them!

It's important to share the heart of God—His intentions—and not just say, "Thou shalt not." So many see our God as a killjoy because they know what He says but not why He says it. Our job is to share the reasons behind God's statements in the Word. We need to present the truth accurately in proper context. God always loves us. We need to help people see that. When He says no to adultery, there's a reason, so we should tell folks what the reason is. We need to show them God is not a power hungry dictator whose goal is to make us miserable. He wants us to be filled with joy, to be safe, and to feel loved. When we teach truth, we have to demonstrate its application. How does this work in real life? What could this look like in *my* life?

Every message must motivate people to action. Every sermon must encourage believers to live an authentic lifestyle of love. Non-Christians know that we all make mistakes. What they need to see is us admitting it. When we fail, we ask forgiveness. When they see us being real, they may respond. The world knows a fake when it sees one. Many stereotype the church as a building full of hypocrites. If we could deal with real issues, as humble, broken, but loving people who are trying to do better, the world will respect that. If unbelievers walk away with the impression of a friendly church, where people genuinely try to love one another, they may want to come back. If all they see is ritual and all they hear is platitudes, they will only know they don't understand, they don't fit, and they can't relate. They won't feel motivated to do anything, including make a return visit to church.

BAPTISMS

At Real Life our goal is to reach the world for Jesus, so we baptize those who were won to Christ in the last week right there in front of our people. It's an "aha moment," where they remember what we are about. We also have the people who were a part of their conversion baptize them. This promotes what we believe about every person being a player, a priest, a minister, with the purpose of declaring the praises of Him who saved us. It's an amazing thing to see people baptize their brother or sister, mother or father, neighbor or classmate. It's a thrill to see home groups come up and baptize someone from their group or to see a single mom baptize a co-worker. People leave thanking God that they got to be used by Him.

DIRECTED PRAYER

During our worship service, we have something we call directed prayer. It's a time where we have someone on stage direct the thoughts of those in the service to a particular person or thing. We then allow a few moments for people to pray silently. For instance, one might be, "If you are not right with God, talk with Him now. He wants to forgive you." Another might be, "Jesus came to seek and to save the lost. Pray for somebody you know who doesn't know Jesus. Ask the Lord what He wants you to do about it."

Others include prayer for a brother or sister in Christ who might be struggling. We encourage them to ask the Lord how He

116

might want to use them to uplift someone else, maybe by making a phone call, sending a note, or taking a meal. Sometimes we pray for special needs in our church, and we pray for our troops who are fighting for us.

We do this for several reasons. First, we want to model prayer for our people. It's important to pray weekly as a church. God has blessed us because we have asked for His guidance, strength, and protection. Second, we want our people to pray for others specifically. I hear every week about a person who has been praying for years for a son or husband or friend who is in our church that day. God has grown our church because our people are constantly praying for people they know. Third, we are programming our people every week to be soul winners. So often people think their job is to bring people to church and the pastor will share Christ with them. This is not biblical. We are all to be involved as the Lord's army to infiltrate a community to intentionally make disciples.

There is one final component: a reminder to our people every week that praying is great, but that God can use them to be an answer to their own prayers. God wants to use each one to share His love with others. Many of our people leave church with the inspiration to act on their prayers. Once again, we have grown spiritually and numerically because everything we do promotes the entire team participating instead of just watching a single paid player.

COMMUNION AND OFFERING

We celebrate communion weekly because we believe we need to be reminded often of the price Jesus Christ paid for us. We want to look at ourselves, at our unworthiness, and remember the Father loves us anyway. Sometimes I preach about family, work, or values, but we think the gospel ought to be taught every Sunday, which is done through communion. Some have said, "Isn't taking communion less meaningful if it's a weekly occurrence?" My response: "Only if you allow it to be so. Is God any less special when you worship every week? Is He any less special when you pray every day?"

Most of our decision cards come in after directed prayer and communion and before the message. At first this puzzled me because I wanted the message to inspire people to make decisions. Yet what I've found is that when you allow people to spend time with God in worship and prayer, reminding them during communion of what Jesus did for them, the Spirit convicts them and they make decisions. There is a difference between being the church and going to church.

THE INVITATION

Though many make decisions before the sermon, we believe that an invitation ought to be given every time we get together in a service. We do this in two ways. First, we have a card in every bulletin where people can either write a prayer request or ask to receive a call from a pastor. The prayer requests are prayed over by the pastoral staff, elders, and prayer team. They also receive a phone call or a handwritten card in the mail letting them know their request has been prayed for. If they want to accept Christ, they can record that on the decision card. They are then contacted, and a time to meet is set up that week.

Many people come forward after services also. Our staff, elders, and prayer team members pray with them or share God's plan for their lives with them. We do not ask them to say a prayer and then walk away; we want them to meet with us because we are called to baptize and teach them. We want to help them learn about what it means to have a relationship with Jesus. We want to make disciples, not just converts.

Every week we encourage small group participation, because it's not God's plan for them to be loner Christians. One of the decisions we encourage them to make is to get involved with a small group. We ask them to let us know on the decision card if they are not connected so we can contact them and help them find a group near them.

THE WATERING HOLE

In every weekend service we also include a Connections Card in the bulletin. We use this to help us determine who wasn't in service so we can check on them. On Sunday evening each ministry department gets a report letting them know who from their team was absent from church that week. Team members, which include pastoral staff, small group coaches, and leaders, then start the process of calling those who didn't make it. We do this because God has said that we should chase the strays (see Ezekiel 34). We know that just because a person misses doesn't mean they have strayed. Sometimes people are sick or on vacation, or they took a day off, and that's okay. However, we believe people are not numbers but are family who appreciate their absence being noticed.

For us, our worship services have another purpose. We see the weekend gathering as a watering hole. Every sheep needs water. Imagine you are a shepherd and you have a fenced field of about a thousand acres with a central watering hole. You can't see the whole field, so rather than chase the sheep, you wait at the watering hole every day. As the sheep come in, you mark their names off the list. You know the sheep need water to survive. If they don't come, you know there can only be a few explanations: (1) they found water somewhere else; (2) they were attacked by a wild animal or are sick; or (3) they broke through the fence and are lost.

We have a flock of about 8,000 who come to five different services, and the Connection Cards help us to shepherd our sheep. Consider a scenario like this: Someone in your church has been missing for months but you never noticed. Then one day they show up at the office with a tear-stained face. Something is terribly wrong. You find out they have been fighting with their spouse, maybe even had an affair. It's a desperate situation, and they inform you that if you can't help, it's over. The situation has developed over time; now it is serious. Hearts are hardened, and you may not be able to help. What if you had been aware of the problem sooner?

VISION AND THE DOOR TO MORE

Every service is a chance to remind our people of what we believe. It not only serves as a reminder but gives newcomers a glimpse of the vision the Lord has given us. Sunday is a chance to let people know what we are about. I can't preach without declaring that we're a small groups, discipleship church and sharing with people how to get connected.

We want those who come to be blessed so they'll want to take the next step of faith. In every service we share what comes next. Our goal is to make them into disciples who disciple others and this happens in small groups.

By vision casting what you are really about in every weekend service, the service becomes a doorway to opportunities for growth and relationships. It's important to provide a variety of options they can select from, get involved in, and stay connected to.

In our bulletins and on our walls, we advertise different ministries and events for people to check out. These are connecting points where people can find places to serve, places to learn, and places to form relationships. In the foyer we have ministry information tables set up that are manned by people ready to welcome a new face. Our leaders are trained to look for the new faces and the not-yet-connected folks and invite them to get in the game.

The corporate worship service is like a pep rally, in many ways. It informs, motivates, and recruits players to join the team or to get out there and get the job done! It rallies us all to win. For the players who are banged up, it's the chance to see a trainer who will get them on their feet again—in other words, we may need to pray with them and love on them.

One of the things we have learned over the years is to use the worship service as a time to promote and praise what you value. If you value service, then praise service. If you value decisions for Jesus, praise those who help people make decisions. If you want people to get connected, then make sure you speak about it often. If you value discipleship, emphasize discipleship. What you value you promote.

A Closer Look at Programs and Events

Every church has its programs, whether they are women's, youth, sports, MOPS (Mothers of Preschoolers), or something else. Programs can be a great team strategy. They provide a place for people to connect, learn, *and* serve. Like any team strategy, a program must be developed to fit within the framework of the team's system. It must have a purpose and fulfill the church's values.

Programs must be interconnected and interdependent with a common goal. Every program in our church has a purpose. They are to take people where they are, teach them, and direct them toward relational discipleship. Every program's leadership must understand its dual purpose in the context of the goal: *winning the world for Jesus, one person at a time, and making disciples in a relational environment.*

The job of a senior high school youth pastor is to take kids from where they are and walk with them further down the path to maturity in Christ. His job is to make sure the students are led through the church's discipleship plan in a relational environment. He must understand that he will be only a *part* of their life's journey. Just as many of these youths were passed on to him from a junior high program, he will in turn hand those he has prepared to the college minister who will develop them further. At each level, the leadership must have done its work so that it benefits the next ministry the person is handed to.

A ministry in our church is a *part* of the process or system we use to meet God's goal. Like the wrestling program we developed in Oregon, beginning with the little guys all the way through the high school, everyone has to be on board. Every program has to have value. Each must be designed to fit players with different backgrounds, needs, interests, and abilities.

Programs are a strategy used in the game; they are *not* the game! Someone with a program mentality is only interested in their own program. They think if they create it, people will come, and when they come, that's it. Job well done! They are satisfied when someone comes to their programmed event as a spectator. They think that if people don't come, it's their problem.

Programmers think in terms of extravaganzas. Now, there's nothing wrong with big events, but their purpose must be to draw people into smaller and smaller relational environments where they can be discipled. At Real Life, we want to build bridges from the event to the desired destination: discipleship.

Every leader in our church understands they are in a shepherding community. They understand they are part of a network of shepherds, all working together to care for the flock. If one of their sheep strays, we will do everything we can to bring them back. If a teen runs away from home, it's not just left to the youth pastor to support the family, because that family may have a mom, a dad, and other kids who are affected. The leaders from other programs have the opportunity to serve and care for those sheep, even if they have not been a part of their care before.

Programs must be about more than just performance. We are instructed to use our gifts and talents to glorify God. Many churches have choirs that produce amazing music. But if our people spend all their time singing beautifully yet are not growing in their understanding of the Word or going deeper with God, we've failed to reach the highest goal. It won't matter if they can hit the right note if they haven't grown in love for one another.

What if the music director knows the purpose of the team and more importantly the Lord's goal for each person? What if the director teaches them to sing, but then in the last half hour they meet in small groups? What if each group has a leader teach a lesson on knowing God, and then they pray together for their marriages, their families, and their concerns? What if they structure choir so they practice and sing only certain times of the year and the rest of the time the groups meet in homes? Real, authentic relationships would start to develop. Accountability would develop. People would grow in their faith.

Our sports leaders have a purpose and a goal as well—to train their coaches to think beyond winning the next game. They initiate team meetings before each game and provide a time of Bible study and prayer. After the game, the coaches pursue intentional relationships with a purpose in mind—to connect these men and women into small groups, to create disciples of Jesus. Softball is the hook, the mutual passion that will draw the participants into relationships that will point them to the *ultimate passion*.

Sometimes a softball coach will spot a player who would make a great small group leader, and he invites him to get involved in learning how to lead.. There is no competition for people between the ministries. He may lose his star player because he got too busy leading a small group. Maybe his team won't be good enough to win. But that's okay; the coach has the right definition of winning.

The team, the whole church, must work together to bring people to the goal. Programs must be designed to make the team win, not to make individuals or certain groups look good. It cannot be solely about performance. If the team works together, they can draw the body together in fellowship or be an effective outreach to the community—and if done right, they both happen!

Events should include everybody on your team. When there is a special community event, we try to include as many of our ministries as possible. During the event, we make it obvious where visitors can get connected. By including the various ministries, we are also providing an opportunity for our people to minister to the community. Our people know the purpose is not to entertain but to lead others to Jesus and get them plugged into where they can be discipled.

Events are not an evangelistic crutch. There is a place for big events, but they must be purposeful. They do not take the place of one-on-one evangelism. They are useful because they give our people something to talk about with their neighbors. They get everyone together for a common purpose, and this creates great excitement. They give people a chance to serve in a beginner's role. They get a taste for service and how it affects people, and they get excited about being used by God to reach the world.

FILLING OUT
THE ROSTER

Players Are Made, Not Born

Every coach, no matter what the level, has a two-tiered job to do: (1) develop skilled players that understand their positions and (2) coach them to play well together.

As I became a part of God's coaching staff, I had to figure out what kind of team I was leading. Was God's team supposed to be a college or a high school program? Let me explain: there are fundamental differences between the two kinds of coaches. Typically, a high school coach is responsible for overseeing a program that extends from the little kids' age group to the high school varsity program. He aligns all the coaches throughout the age groups to produce athletes who understand the style of play expected when the athlete hits the varsity program. A high school coach knows he

125

has no money to give as an incentive to play. He leads a volunteer organization. To win he must develop his own players.

A college coach also develops players, but he deals with athletes who already have a skill base developed by past coaches and experiences. He travels all over the country finding these nearly finished products for his team. If a coach can get the best players, he will have a team that can win— winning teams fill seats.

I believe most leaders of churches behave like college coaches, looking for stars that can be plugged in immediately with little or no development. Jesus, on the other hand, taught His future coaches to work like good high school coaches. God's coaches are to prepare or equip the people for service. We are to develop the gifts and talents of our players and teach them to play as a team.

PLAYERS ARE MADE

The difference in philosophies was best illustrated for me about year two of the Real Life adventure. I was meeting with a pastor who had started a church about the same time we had. We had grown quickly, but his church was struggling. I asked him if he had a group of men he was training for ministry. He explained that he and twenty-three men had been meeting for a year and a half.

I asked if he was allowing them to break into groups and start putting into practice what he had been teaching them. He hadn't. When I asked why not, he said that they were not ready. I gave him a small piece of paper and asked him to write down all they needed to know before he would release them to ministry. He began to write, and five minutes later he was still writing. He even asked for another piece of paper before he was done. He had every subject under the sun on those little pieces of paper; it looked like a seminary master's degree program. At that point, I shared with him how his philosophy was hindering his people and thus the growth of the church.

This kind of thinking results in people feeling like they will never be qualified to serve in any leadership capacity. They don't know what the pastor knows, and they certainly can't teach the way he teaches. They believe that ministry is teaching like their seminary-trained pastor, so they think they have nothing to contribute. In a sense, we are telling them they can't, instead of they can. I believe God wants His church to be a "you can" place.

Our team at Real Life has had the blessing of providing a conference for churches from around the nation. We design our conference to illustrate that God uses everyone to further his purposes. When churches come in, I do the introduction and then the staff proceeds to work with the churches. I go about my usual weekly business as the seminar goes on. At the last session of the conference, I come in to do the conclusion and send-off.

I ask the visiting teams what they think about what they have learned. After meeting with the RLM staff for two and a half days, these leaders say things like, "The reason we cannot succeed the way you do is that we do not have the leaders that you have at your church." Some say, "We wish we had men and women like yours." The truth is, God wants every church to work where they are as much as He wants it to work where we are. His plan will work if we will just work His plan.

At the end of our time together, I prove my point by sharing with these churches the backgrounds and credentials of our staff. Lance was a Mongolian BBQ chef, Brandon worked in a medical office, Gene was an employee for AT&T, Greg worked at a lumber mill as a saw filer, Doug was a mechanic, Ron was a police officer, Jim was a cabinet maker, Genette was a secretary, and Sandy was a social worker. Most have not had any formal training, let alone attended seminary.

My point is that these other churches do have leaders. They have men and women just like ours who would or could become leaders, but have never had the chance. They sit in pews every Sunday. Maybe they sit because their coaches have forgotten their mandate to develop their people. Many potential leaders keep sitting, perhaps, because they are waiting for an invitation.

Consider the people Jesus chose to follow Him. Almost every disciple was unprepared and unqualified. Jesus loves to use people others would bypass. He loves to develop people to be more than anyone thought they could be so He gets the glory.

As I scan America's athletic coaches, I see some who I want to emulate. Mike Krzyzewski of Duke has not only created a dynasty in college basketball but now faces teams led by coaches he taught to play. He still loves those men and is proud of those he had the opportunity to influence. Mike is a great coach! We can also look at Dan Gable, the face of American wrestling. He has influenced many coaches, including some of my own.

The apostle Paul was a great coach too. Read his letters to Timothy. He trained him, released him, and then said, "Do as I did for you." He compelled others to train reliable men who would be able to train others. Good coaches delight in raising up great players who will become the great coaches of tomorrow.

GOLD MINES IN OUR MIDST

Sometimes coaches are so busy looking for the mega leader they miss many potential gold mines sitting right in front of them. God has capable, godly people in every Bible-believing congregation. If you develop them, they can be great players and eventually great leaders. If you expect to receive skilled players out of the blue, you will usually be disappointed. Occasionally, such a player will move in, but you can't count on that. We must help people to know and believe that God has gifted everyone for some position on the team. The devil works hard to tell each person he or she is no good or is too good. A good coach knows how to deal with each player accordingly.

Many kinds of abilities are useful to a team. In our church, we have a young man, Daniel Spencer, who is a typical computer guy. He loves to work on his computer and is kind of quiet. I think he would say that he is better with computers than with people, but he has a heart to serve God. Daniel has started a youth Local Area Network (LAN) small group in our church. We gave him computers to use, and he started inviting kids just like him, kids who love computers. They order pizza, get their computers interfaced, and play games all night at the church.

Kids have come to Christ because of LAN. These kids didn't go to our youth group, but they have now found a place where they belong and can relate. Most importantly, they have effectively been bridged from LAN to Jesus. LAN became a relational environment for discipleship.

Daniel might not be the usual player, but God brought him, and he was trained and invited to be on the team. He has proven to be an effective leader. Thank God some of our leaders spotted him, recognized his potential, and put him in the game!

❖

Are you looking for the right things when you look for leaders? Are you looking for people who have a heart to serve, or are you looking for people who love the spotlight? Are you looking for teachable people with different gifts and asking, "How can God use those gifts on the field?" Or do you have two categories—great showmen and spectators? I believe there are leaders in every church. A good coach finds them and inspires them to be used for God's glory.

09

IN THE HUDDLE

The Essential Role of Small Groups

If you want to be a great coach, you must look at what great coaches do. The best way to become like them is to watch them, listen to them, and mimic them.

Jesus is the best example of what it means to be a great coach. He gave us a picture of real discipleship that works. Unlike many pastors today, Jesus knew that you cannot disciple in mass numbers. Yes, He spoke to the crowds, but He took His disciples aside and taught them in a relational way. Discipleship is a process that can only be accomplished through relationship. Jesus was the master of effective education. He taught in a small group.

Imagine that you had a child whom you loved more than life. Like all parents, you wanted this child to grow to be a positive influence on the human race. Let's say that your child has to pass geometry with at least a C to get into college. If he doesn't get a degree from a college, he cannot get a job, and without a job, he cannot support a family. In the high school that your child attends, they have chosen to teach geometry in a classroom that holds five hundred kids. The teacher stands in front of the crowd and does geometry problems on the board.

The teacher tries her best to explain how to answer the problems for thirty-five minutes one time a week and then dismisses the class. She does not have time to meet in private tutoring sessions, and she does not have a method to help students who are struggling. She tells you when you question her that the students have the book—they should just read it. How would you feel about the school your child goes to, especially since so much is riding on the grade? When I give this scenario to loving parents and they imagine it happening to their child, it makes their blood boil. Of course they would never stand for such a thing.

Why do we react so adversely to this but allow the same type of thing to happen in our churches every week? The people in our pews are struggling with the most important subject there is—salvation. We stand in front of them for forty minutes a week and describe on the big screen what it takes to solve life's biggest problems. We don't have time to tutor them, and we don't raise up people who do. Is it any wonder why our people can't answer the easiest of biblical questions?

How much more is riding on how well God's children understand the Scriptures and apply them to their lives? We must remember that God's Word is truth and that the gospel is the means of our salvation. It is also our guide to a fulfilling life. This can only be passed on through a relational discipleship process. God's plan included those who would guide people to maturity. It cannot be done in a forty-minute lecture once a week any more than geometry can be taught to a large group in forty minutes per week. Why do we accept in the church what we would never accept in a classroom with our own kids?

So what does true discipleship really look like? What components must be included in the discipleship process that in the end will lead to a mature disciple who is able to disciple another?

REAL DISCIPLESHIP INCLUDES REAL TEACHING

Educators are always trying to figure out how to better teach our kids. Most educators recognize that the success of a civilization is often tied to its abilities in the classroom. Recently, many have noted the decline in test scores for American students in the most important subjects, i.e., math, science, and history. At least one of the causes, experts have discovered, is a lack of good teachers.

When George Bush became president, he sought to remedy that problem with the No Child Left Behind policy. As I have spoken to teachers, I have found that even good teachers struggle with the results of the program. They know that only a small percentage of students learn best through a lecture style of teaching. The problem is, the larger the classroom size, the more it forces teachers to lecture. The teachers get frustrated because, if students do not learn the material, the teachers will lose their job. The problem: kids are crammed into the classrooms and the teachers are forced to use what does not work. The teacher, good or bad, loses his or her job, the kids don't learn, and the system fails.

Why is it that teachers have discovered something pastors have not? Why do pastors think they are successful because they have thousands come to listen to them speak when good teachers would see it as a major problem? If you were to test Christians who attend churches in America on their understanding of the Bible, you would discover quickly that they are not learning. Statisticians have sought to test that statement and the results are interesting, to say the least. I discuss this more later.

As a teacher, I learned to value small class sizes. A good teacher, in the right setting, can get to know each student. In other words, in a "relational environment," a teacher can really teach each student. The teacher can discover what learning style a student has, how a new principle applies to a student's life, and when a student isn't getting it. A good teacher will also recognize when a child is going through a difficult time outside the classroom and can come alongside the child and help them deal with the life issue immediately. It will do no good to teach American history to a student whose parents are divorcing or who is being mistreated. The teacher can also earn the right to be heard later by how he deals with the situation right then.

As we look at Scripture, we can see Jesus's teaching style. When Jesus taught, He told stories people could relate to. He asked questions to test their understanding and lead them further. Christ taught not only with words, He modeled for them the behaviors He wanted to see in them. When dealing with our children, we often hear that *character is caught, not taught.* Jesus modeled everything from how to deal with enemies to how to deal with sinners. He modeled how to love and serve and fight. He modeled humility, love, and righteous anger. Discipleship includes theology, but Jesus taught much more. Jesus chose twelve disciples and created a small group—because in small groups people can really learn. If there were a better way to teach, He would have shown it to us.

DISCIPLESHIP INCLUDES ACCOUNTABILITY

Accountability involves a relationship based on honesty, love, and trust. We all need someone in our life who will say the hard things. Scripture encourages us to "seek wise counsel" and to "heed reproof." Proverbs 18:1 tells us, "He who separates himself seeks *his own* desire, he quarrels against all sound wisdom" (NASB, emphasis added).

Few of us have accountability in our relationships. It takes time to build a relationship, especially one that allows others to know us well enough to speak truth to our hearts. I have seen many pastors fall because they hid from those who could help them in times of weakness.

I learned a lot about myself when dealing with my drinking problem in the late 1980s. Alcoholics Anonymous (AA) had it right and many churches had it wrong. I felt weak and alone, though I had given my life to Christ. Most of the Christians I knew kept to themselves. Oh, there were potlucks where a lot of small talk occurred but not a lot of sharing about failings. Sometimes there was a lot of theological banter and some gossip about the pastor's kids, but nothing real. Maybe because they believed they had to appear holy. If anyone really knew them, the truth of who they are would come out. They're imperfect, just like everybody else. We all struggle. The devil wants us to believe we are the only ones dealing with a specific problem. He loves to get us alone and tell us we are horrible, or that we have it worse than anyone else so we are somehow justified in our behavior. So, we live alone in the dark where the devil loves to play.

During my struggle with alcoholism, I discovered a verse that has become my life verse: "See to it . . . that none of you has a sinful, unbelieving heart that turns away from the living God. But encourage one another daily . . . so that none of you may be hardened by sin's deceitfulness" (Heb. 3:12–13). This passage reveals that we are called to *encourage*. As I studied the definition of this word, I found that it means to build up or to root another on in the race! But it also means to admonish. We are to be with people who will tell us the truth, what we need to hear even if it isn't what we want to hear. God says to do this *daily* because He knows we can get messed up in the head in a moment's time. We need constant support. When I know a person loves me, I will allow them to say the hard things. When someone really knows me, I don't have the excuse that they just misunderstood what I said or did. Only in relationship can we accept the advice, counsel, and admonishment as real and from a loving heart.

Unfortunately, all I found in church at the time was a place to go once a week. I had many questions, but no one to answer them. The pastor was too busy and no one else had time. AA became essential in my life. The church wasn't there to help, so the secular world stepped in.

Jesus modeled effective discipleship for us through building relationships. He could call His disciples on the carpet when they got it wrong. He encouraged them and provided a safe place where they could voice their shortcomings and ask for help. He had a small group of men He could really know and thus keep accountable. Once again, real discipleship happens in small groups.

DISCIPLESHIP REQUIRES AUTHENTICITY

A discipleship environment must include authenticity. Churches can be full of pretentious people trying to make an impression. If everyone is a fake, there can be no accountability. Church relationships are then shallow and superficial. Discipleship must provide a safe place to share your struggles without rejection. When someone asks, "How are you doing?" it's okay to say, "Not so good." When you know someone is struggling, then you can come alongside to help.

Before I was a Christian, I only went to church if a girl I was interested in invited me. I remember my thoughts like they were yesterday. I would listen to the preacher and think, "That guy is really good if he can do everything he is preaching about all the time. I could never be like him, so why try?" Or I'd think, "That guy is a hypocrite; he's pretending to be good on stage!" Either way, I didn't want to be there.

Many have discovered that church is not a safe place to be real. They may have experienced a ruined reputation, caused by gossip after a moment of honesty occurred in the wrong setting. Maybe the problem was shared in a prayer circle—for their own good, of course. Then the gossip hits the prayer chain. These unfortunate events lead people to deal with their issues alone, without the love and encouragement of another believer, without the body.

Before people will be real, they must see their leader be real. This doesn't mean we constantly air our dirty laundry, but we let others know that we struggle, we fall, and we keep trying. In James 5:16, we are told that we can find healing when we confess our sins to one another. If our kids see us fight all the way to church and then put on a happy face as soon as we walk in the church, they'll think, "Oh, this is a place you have to be perfect to attend" or "This is the place where you must put on a mask."

I would rather ask how someone is doing and hear, "Not good, but I'm here," or hear them say that they fought all the way to church and need prayer. That is real! Kids will then learn it is okay to admit their struggles to those they trust at church. They will learn where real power is found. Real discipleship includes authenticity. In small groups, people can really know you and how you struggle. They can see you deal with things honestly and know it is okay to live without masks.

DISCIPLESHIP INCLUDES TEACHING AND RELEASING

When it comes to playing a game or learning a trade, you can learn only so much in a classroom or on the bench watching the game. Those who just sit never become great athletes or great at a job. In the early church, the disciples put new Christians in minor leadership roles, like the deacons in charge of caring for the widows in Acts 6. They were given the responsibility to serve, and as they did, they grew. Philip started out meeting people's physical needs and became a great evangelist—spreading the gospel to Samaria and Ethiopia.

If our goal is to make disciples who can disciple others, we must release them into the field of ministry. Jesus modeled this when He sent out the seventy-two to preach in the area towns. He then brought them back to debrief their experiences. He did this more than once because He knew you can only go so far until you get the chance to use what you are learning.

We learn by doing. The job of a disciple maker is to teach and release so that those being taught can truly learn. In wrestling, my job as a coach was to teach a wrestling move by demonstrating it while the kids watched. I then broke the kids into groups and allowed them to do the move repeatedly. I also was responsible for setting up the schedule with the area schools so that our kids could compete against other wrestlers. The true test was whether or not our kids could do what they had learned in a live situation on their own.

In the same sense, the job of a coach is to provide a place for the athletes to practice what they learn and eventually do it in their own life. My best kids would stick around and help me coach the elementary, junior high, and JV wrestlers in our own program. Eventually, some became coaches of their own school programs. A good coach provides a place for the students to play. Speaking in front of and leading thousands or even hundreds is so scary; it is a skill set that requires specific gifting. Learning to speak in front of or lead a small group is still scary, but it is something that almost anyone can be taught to do. Jesus used small groups because He wanted to raise up the regular guy to be a part of His movement to reach the world.

METHOD MATTERS

As an evangelical Christian, I know there is only one way to attain salvation: through Jesus Christ. Only He can save us from our sins, having paid the price for them when He died on the cross. Only the Spirit of God can change selfish humans with no hope, into people who can have a relationship with God and with others. The Scriptures tell us if you add to or take away from God's Word, you are outside the will of God. I would go so far as to say that those who change, minimize, or distort the gospel are in danger of hell (see Gal. 1:6–8).

I can say confidently there is a reason churches that have strayed from the Word of God are not growing: they have lost the blessing of God. If those who distort the Word of God *are* growing, it will be short lived. There will be a cost beyond which no one will care to pay. The Word of God is central to our understanding of the world, eternity, and salvation.

Many pastors in America would agree with what I have just said when it pertains to right theology. However, when it comes to the church, what it does and is, they believe they can come up with any method they want and still be within the will of God. Many strategies for winning and training disciples have sprung up in recent years. Most of them are in response to the busy world in which we live. Though the intentions are good and right, the result is usually not discipleship. There are Internet churches where people don't have to leave their homes. While they reach people who are truly shut-ins because of health reasons, they are also designed to make life easier for people. Rather than calling for a life change, it seems like the goal becomes making church convenient.

Jesus calls us to follow Him and take up our cross daily. God's Word tells us to seek after His kingdom and His righteousness, and to stop chasing the things of the world. Instead, some try to take the gospel message and package it in a way that is compatible with the American lifestyle and culture, regardless of whether it's what God wants. We must reach people *where they are*, but that doesn't mean we make it easy for them to stay there.

The God who tells us in His Word how to be saved is the same God who outlines how to disciple someone effectively. The Book that tells us what sin is teaches that discipleship is a process that only works in relationship. In other words, a church can preach the right message in the wrong way and lose the power to change lives. God created the church to spread the Good News in the best way—discipleship. His plan bridges generational and historical differences.

Pastors are trying their best to preach the gospel but are employing a model for discipleship that doesn't work. As a result, they are producing the wrong product—church-attending Christians who live like the rest of the world.

The other day I heard someone say, "It's a sign of the times. That's why the church in America is in such horrible shape." Maybe we do have a hard-hearted generation. Maybe we are in the end times. After all, Jesus said that in the end people would become lovers of themselves instead of God; they would always be learning but never believing. But I also believe that we have not helped the situation much. I think we need to go back to God's model, the discipleship system outlined in Scripture. Let's go back to building godly leaders through His relational discipleship process—small groups. With more godly leaders building disciples, we will have more followers, more shepherding, more teaching, and more changed lives.

A PICTURE IN ACTS

In Acts 2:41–47, the people were devoted to something. They had purpose and meaning in a world that appeared to lack a cause. In a selfish and lonely world, they bonded together for something greater than themselves. They had everything in common, selling their possessions and goods in order to give to whoever had need. The result was a church regarded with favor by the world. They saw people who loved and served one another. Rather than pointing fingers at each other and judging everyone else, they were generous givers. How can anyone dislike those who give generously? An unbeliever may not receive the gospel but may say, "You know what? The people in that church helped me when I was down."

It all starts with the gospel, but then we must apply the right methodology to see God's power change a community. There must be a design, a framework, for this to take place. The design is the church's strategies for implementing the discipleship plan.

The result of the discipleship process in a community is growth. When a church works as a team, they develop people—people who look like Jesus. It's those who have found living water, wholeness, and purpose who will take over a community for Jesus. In other words, if we teach biblical truths and principles, and use Jesus's discipleship methods, it will produce people who stand out in the world rather than go along with it.

THE CHAMPIONSHIP
PROGRAM

*A Reproducible Strategy
for Leadership Development*

Many churches come to Real Life believing they are making disciples. After hearing our definition of what a disciple is and our method and reason for making disciples, they are often somewhat unsure whether they really have been doing what they thought they were doing. In the cases where pastors have an accurate definition of discipleship, they discover that their team rarely has a shared idea or definition to work from. It seems everyone has their own idea and consequently are doing their own thing.

As we have worked with churches over the last few years, we have consistently gotten two questions.

THE DEFINITION OF A DISCIPLE

The first question is "What is a disciple?" To answer this, we point them to Matthew 4:18–20 where we read,

> As Jesus was walking beside the Sea of Galilee, he saw two brothers, Simon called Peter and his brother Andrew. They were casting a net into the lake, for they were fishermen. "Come, follow me," Jesus said, "and I will make you fishers of men." At once they left their nets and followed him.

So four things define a disciple:

First, a *disciple is one who has made Jesus the Lord of his or her life.* Jesus said, "Come, and follow me." He is the leader. We must be committed to being the followers.

Second, *a disciple is one who has entered a process of relational discipleship with other maturing Christians.* Jesus invited His disciples to be in relationship with Him. It was the primary way He shaped them. Later, in Matthew 28:19, Jesus told His disciples to go and make disciples. In other words, "Go and help people become what I helped you become." Discipleship was intended to be a process shared with other believers. We are to be in a relationship with one who will help us grow, and we are to be in relationships with others who will need our help as well.

Third, *a disciple is one who is becoming Christlike.* He or she has begun a process of change that is orchestrated by Jesus. Jesus said, "Come, follow me, and I will make you" . . . into something. He transforms us, reshapes us, into Christlikeness by the power of the Holy Spirit and the Word of God. God is making each one of us into a "little Jesus" who will have the fruit of the Spirit.

Finally, *a disciple is one who is committed to the mission of Christ.* Jesus said that He would make us into "fishers of men." When we spend time with Jesus, we start to care about what He cares about. Jesus came to seek and to save the lost. We have joined His mission to save the world.

Jesus created everyone with specific talents, and the Holy Spirit gives each disciple a gift supernaturally (see Rom. 12; 1 Cor. 12). Jesus will use this gift in His mission to reach the world. This gift is to be used by each of us as we walk through life, and it is to be used as a part of a team so that the church can do together more than any one individual could do alone. Church is a team sport.

An Intentional Process for Reproducing Discipleship

The second question we are often asked is "What is the reproducible process you use to make disciples?" We call it the Share, Connect, Minister, and Disciple process, or S.C.M.D. for short (see pages 157–58).

As I stated earlier, many who visit Real Life believe they are making disciples by teaching, which is usually defined by them as the transfer of information in a teaching or preaching setting. They define maturity based on knowledge. But after we've defined discipleship differently for those who visit, they want to know how to do it. They want to know how to reproduce the process so they can be a part of a discipleship movement.

As a team, we have identified four phases or stages of discipleship. Each stage is a necessary part of the process. In other words, you cannot get to the fourth stage without going through the first three. No one stage is better than any other; they are just a way we have been able to measure where people are so that we can help them grow. There are lessons to learn in each phase. Schools do this to measure the twelve grades a child must go through to graduate. This is a leader-directed process. In other words, Disciple-level leaders guide those they lead through the process. We want our disciples to understand the process because we want discipleship to be reproducible. When you intentionally release people who understand how to make disciples of Jesus, it is reproducible and becomes a movement rather than a church. When people believe they can and should make disciples, growth becomes exponential.

Share

We call the first stage the *Share* phase. Share-level people are those who have either not accepted Jesus as Lord and Savior or have accepted Him but have not been connected to other believers. Obviously, at this point those who have not accepted Christ need to hear, understand, and commit themselves to the Lord and His gospel. Unsaved people need salvation. We then want to connect them into a relational environment for discipleship. Those who have already accepted Christ but have not been connected to other believers need to be connected as well. Everyone needs to be discipled. Discipleship is a relational process.

Connect

Once disciples have entered the *Connect* phase of the process, the leader and the group they connect with will inspire, teach, and model for them what it means to love God and others. In their small group there will be many lessons and many questions answered so that the Connect-level people are growing in their knowledge of the Word. A proper disciple-led Connect environment should eventually result in heart change as the group studies the Word and prays together. In the meantime, the Connect-level disciples are going to church, taking some Bible classes, and reading books that will bolster their understanding of what it means to be a Christian.

Minister

People who are properly connected and have the right heart will eventually start to move into the *Ministry* phase of discipleship. In this stage they will start to see things as God sees them, because they are connected to Him. As they grow spiritually, they will become more and more committed to the mission of Christ. Hopefully, they will have had a model of service in their small group. They will see it in others in the church family. They will hear about it from the pulpit. They will read about it in the Word. The Holy Spirit will be changing them as they are growing spiritual fruit in their lives. When they walk into a room, rather than thinking, *Who will talk to me? Who is going to notice me?* they are being transformed into people who think, *Who needs help? He looks lonely.* They become other-centered people, servants, a natural result of walking with the Lord.

Disciple

Finally, the young disciples will move into the last stage of the discipleship process. We call this the *Disciple* phase. In this stage the disciples learn not only to minister to those around them but to train others to do the same thing. Disciple-level leaders now provide the new Disciple-level people with opportunities to lead by connecting them with others who need to be discipled. Eventually they will no longer need to be fed people because they will connect with others on their own. The new Disciple-level people have become leaders who can guide others through the same process they just came through. Consequently, their leaders become peers who encourage their one-time students to continue to walk with Christ. The relationship changes from teacher/pupil to friend—those with whom they serve.

COACHING PRINCIPLES

In wrestling, I had kids at all different levels on my team. My job was to figure out where each guy was and put together a plan to help him attain the next level of his development. I did not train each guy the same way, because what would help one person would hurt another. By the same token, what would help one might bore another to death. A good coach develops a plan that helps each person attain the next level of their development and then helps his coaches understand the process so they can develop the ability to do the same with others. First things first, you must be able to recognize where each person is. In sports it's easy—just watch them at practice and in the game. In discipleship you must both watch and listen while providing a place for them to "play." What they do does not by itself determine where they are. Many do the right things for the wrong reasons, but mature disciples will try to do the right thing for the right reason. Therefore, you must watch people "in action" and then listen to why they do what they do. This can only be accomplished through the proximity of relationship.

PHRASE FROM THE PHASE

Part of the Disciple-level leaders' job is to be able to recognize when and how God is working in another person's life. The Lord brings people into our lives who are at different levels of growth spiritually. As Disciple-level leaders, we must understand the game well enough to identify where a person is in the process. For instance, some are not Christians but God is drawing them; some gave their lives to Jesus at some point but have never been discipled, so they are very immature in their faith. Others are Christians who are struggling and need encouragement; still others are Christians who need to learn a lesson. The key is to determine who needs what.

The team at Real Life created a way to help leaders recognize where people are. The key is to ask questions and listen—to listen to the *phrase from the phase*. Remember, the phases in the process are Share, Connect, Minister, and Disciple. At each phase of the process, people say things that tell us where they are. Once we know where they are, we as leaders can help get them what they need for growth.

SHARE-LEVEL PEOPLE

There are different kinds of Share-level people—the unsaved and the saved. When unsaved people are at the Share level, we know what they need—they need salvation, they need the gospel. We may take them through the biblical evidences, or we may answer questions they have had for a long time. In this phase, they also need an understanding of what it means to be a Christian—to know what the expectations are, why they can trust Christ, and what's next. They need to be led in the right direction. That is why God's plan is to bring them into relationship with believers.

Recently saved people usually have misconceptions about what Christianity is and what Jesus will do for them. They may believe God is the genie of the Bible—they just need to rub the Bible and they will get three wishes. They may believe Christians will always be nice to each other. They don't understand that now, as believers, they have the potential to be powerful adversaries against the devil, and therefore, he has declared war on them. The new believers need Disciple-level leaders who will give them some basic knowledge and will share about the habits that need to be developed. The best thing for them is to be in relationship with a more mature believer who will walk beside them.

Share-level people who have been believers for a while are a little trickier to understand. They may have "prayed the prayer" years ago and may even know the Bible inside and out and have all the right answers, but they are missing the will of God by not being connected and involved. It doesn't matter how many degrees from Bible college a person has, how many verses they can quote, or if they are a pastor of a church. If people are not in relation-ships with other believers for the purpose of growth, fulfillment, and protection, they are Share-level people. They have missed the point of the entirety of Scripture, summed up in loving God and loving one another.

Phrase from the Phase

Let's look at phrases used by a couple kinds of Share-level people. Those who are unsaved may say things like, "I don't believe in the Bible," or "I believe Jesus is a way to get to heaven but He is not the only way," or "I went to church when I was young, but Christians were mean to my family, so we never went back." Other phrases may include: "What do I need to be saved for? I am as good as anyone else." They may want to talk to us about *The Da Vinci Code, The Secret*, or evolution. Their questions may range from "How do you know Jesus is real?" to "Why does God allow bad things to happen?" I am not saying as leaders we will have all the answers, but now we know God has brought them into our lives to reach them or to grow us—either way, we know where they are at. We are able to recognize the "phrase from the phase." In each case we know that they have never accepted Jesus as Lord and Savior of their lives.

At this point we can start to answer questions and begin a relationship. Remember that Jesus was always looking for the one looking for Him. Zacchaeus is a great example. He had climbed the tree, trying to see Jesus. Jesus recognized his need and his effort, and He joined God the Father to bring salvation to Zacchaeus's house.

Another kind of Share-level people are those who have accepted Jesus as Savior, as the Son of God, but have not understood what Jesus says about others believers and the Church, or have just flat-out rebelled against it. We will recognize these people by what they say. The phrase from the phase will be something like this: "I love Jesus, but *my* church is in the mountains [meadows, nature] because I feel close to God there," or "I have been hurt too many times by believers to let them get too close to me," or "My accountability partner is God." Another phrase that's often used is "I am too busy at work to get connected."

The phrase tunes us into the phase. If it is true they love God but will not adjust their lives to His priorities, then they are not very spiritually mature. They may be Christians, but they are spiritual infants in need of growth.

CONNECT-LEVEL PEOPLE

Connect-level people are those who have moved into a group led by a Disciple-level person (best-case scenario). They are in a relational environment for the purpose of discipleship. If the group is functioning correctly, these groups act like little churches. People learn from one another and love each other while helping to take care of the needs in the group. Connect-level people serve the church as a whole in many ways.

Within their small groups, people are known individually, questions are answered, prayer is modeled, and time is spent growing spiritually with church family. They are starting to learn who they are in Christ. They are learning basic theology as they are led through the Bible in their groups.

People in this level may even be involved in ministry, but they will serve because they want to be a part of something or because they are still working from a works-salvation mind-set. They serve out of fear (to be good enough for God), because everyone else is doing it (peer pressure), because they get some emotional charge from it, or because it gives them some clout. They will often serve with "me" motives. If this is the case, they will usually continue to serve as long as the benefits outweigh the challenges.

Again, there is nothing wrong with people being in the Connect stage of development for a time unless a Connect-level person is in a Ministry-level or Disciple-level leadership position. If this is the case, they will keep many in their group from progressing past the Connect phase because they are the example—a group will rarely grow past its leader. Instead, the whole group will become "me" thinkers instead of servants. Connect-level leaders typically develop clubs, not ministries or biblical churches. At this level the flesh is too involved for this person to be in a position of leadership. More mature Christians will avoid the Connect-led ministry because they can see the flesh is the motivation for service. These kinds of ministries are time bombs waiting to go off in the church and in the lives of the individuals involved. Nothing of real spiritual substance can be accomplished in a ministry led by a Connect-level person.

Phrase from the Phase

As Disciple-level leaders, we will recognize that many Connect-level people in our group will be growing but will often be consumed with self. They still often have a "me" mentality. Their language often contains phrases like these: "I love my group." "I have never felt so loved." "I finally found home." Notice the "I" word over and over again. There is nothing wrong with this at the Connect stage. They should love their group: it may be the first time they have ever felt loved in their lives.

A self-centered attitude may also surface in comments like these: "The leaders better not try to branch [split] my group—I was just starting to get comfortable here," or "I had to walk a hundred yards to get into church last Sunday. It made me so mad." They might also say, "I was working in the nursery, but they don't appreciate me there, so I think I am going to quit." My favorite is, "I am not comfortable at that church. There are far too many people." Did you notice the emphasis on self?

MINISTRY-LEVEL PEOPLE

Remember, a Ministry-level person is one who has made the transition from "I" to "others." They will seek to do what they do so that God will be glorified. They are also interested in serving in a ministry for more than what they can get out of it. When asked why they serve, they reply, "Hey, the Lord saved me. It's the least I can do for Him." They will stick with it even when they face the downside of ministry.

This is the time for us as disciple makers to challenge our Ministry-level people to grow in their understanding of the Word in new ways. We might suggest a class at the church that will equip them for ministry. We might recommend a book to read. In many of our groups at Real Life, the leaders may start a new group for their people who want to go deeper. We also encourage our Disciple-level leaders to look for an apprentice and begin to train them to lead a future group. A Ministry-level person is a perfect candidate for such a job.

Once we see there has been a change in the heart of Connect-level people, we know that they have moved into the Ministry phase of the process. It's time to start training the Ministry-level people to minister with the gifts and talents the Lord has given them. We, as Disciple-level leaders, have been the example, but now we start to help the Ministry-level people know how to apply the Scriptures to their own lives and the lives of others. We teach them to actually get into the game themselves and help them find the place to do it. Opportunities to share their faith and help people are everywhere, when they open their eyes and care for others. Of course, the best place to start is in their own family, work environment, or school environment, so we will encourage them to be other-centered in the world they live in first.

Later, we may get them connected into a ministry position within the church. We may make them apprentices in our small groups. We may get them connected with the hospital team or the youth group. We will try to help the Ministry-level people discern their passions and giftings, and try to point them in the right direction.

Ministry-level people will need guidance. The job of Disciple-level leaders is not only to move these young disciples into opportunities to serve but also to provide encouragement and help as they stumble through the first-time opportunities. These new ministers will often feel completely over their heads and will need constant uplifting.

Phrase from the Phase

So far we have looked at the Share and Connect phases of the process. Now let's look at the Ministry phase closely. Remember that the Connect-level person uses the words "I" and "me" a lot. We know where they are by listening to the phrase from the phase. They are self focused. This is OK; that is where they should be for a time. However, we will start to notice a change in some of the people in the group. They will start to use language that is distinctly different. Rather than talking about their group, or their gifts, they will start to become other centered in their language. For instance, they will start to talk about people in their group:

"I wonder where Megan is tonight. Does anyone know why she isn't here? I was watching her the other day and she seems kind of down. I was thinking about making her a meal and taking it over." Their heart for others begins coming out in what they do. When talk of branching their group starts, we will hear them talk about how much the group has helped them, and how everyone needs a group like this. They will be the ones who say, "We need to make room even though it is hard." They are the ones in our groups who are sharing stories about how they got the chance to share Christ with someone at their work. They come up to us at church and say, "Isn't this amazing! I had to sit way in the back this week. The parking lot is totally full and I had to walk for ten minutes. Isn't this awesome!"

The people in this level become compassionate when someone is hurting in the group. They start calling missing people on their own. They have come to the place where they realize that life is not all about them but about glorifying God. They are becoming a giver rather than a taker, a servant for the right reasons. They don't want to be a part of a club; they want to see people cared for and loved. At this point they have become people who serve not to get but because they have experienced the love of Jesus and they want others to experience it too. They do what they do for Jesus, whether they get anything for it or not. They have become Ministry-level people—by "minister," I mean those who are caring for the needs of others. They have become servants. This does not mean that they don't struggle with the flesh, or that they don't sink into "me" thinking—we all do at times, no matter how long we have been a Christian. However, at this level they recognize it and begin to seek the Lord's help in putting that part of themselves to death.

DISCIPLE-LEVEL PEOPLE

Before too long, people in the Ministry level will desire to do more than care for a need. They will begin to ask questions like, "Who can I get to help me reach more people in this ministry?"

When we as their Disciple-level leader notice Ministry-level people desire to train others, it's time to help develop a strategy. Paul did this with Timothy when he said, "Do what you have seen me do." Train our disciples to train others.

Notice that our goal is to raise up those who can make disciples. Disciples learn as they go. They do not have to be perfect to get into the game, because perfection is not possible. Getting good at a game you don't play is not possible either. Our method for raising up people is through small groups. In those small groups, our leaders have access to people. They can start to know them well enough to really teach them, and they can see their talents and walk beside them as they develop them. They can give them opportunities to lead with the Disciple-level person present. This gives the leaders the ability to debrief them and walk beside them. Finally, the new Disciple-level person is able to lead a group themselves.

In our church every ministry and small group is under the supervision of a full-time staff pastor and a volunteer coach. There is communication between the small group leader, the volunteer coach, and the pastor of that ministry to determine where, when, and how a new Disciple-level person will start to lead a group of their own.

Phrase from the Phase

The question here is, how do we know when a Ministry-level person is ready to move to the Disciple level? Again, we must listen to the phrase from the phase. We will hear them say something like, "Have you noticed Sam? He is really talented with those kids; he should be using those gifts for the Lord." Or they might say, "I have been going to the hospital to pray for our older folks, and I was thinking about taking George with me. He is so compassionate and loves to pray. I thought I would show him what you showed me and maybe we could pray with twice as many people in a shorter time."

Notice a few things. First, Disciple-level people see the need to grow a ministry they are passionate about. Second, they notice that the ministry could expand if they had help. Third, they notice the gifts and passions of someone else who could play a part in the ministry. Fourth, they are willing to invest in another who they see needs to be trained. They believe that they and their friends can serve and that it is their responsibility and privilege to train them so they can serve. A Disciple-level person wants to share the joy of serving with others by giving them the opportunity as well.

CATCH AND RELEASE: THE KEY TO GROWTH

We have all heard the saying, "If you give someone a fish, you feed them for a day; if you teach them to fish, they will feed themselves for life." The main objective of discipleship is to bring everyone to the Disciple level where they have learned to minister with another purpose: to train others to do the same things they have been taught to do. God's ultimate goal is for us to glorify Him. We do this by doing what He has called and empowered us to do. Disciples reproduce disciples. Some disciple one-on-one with a friend, a spouse, or children, while others disciple in small groups. Still others God uses to create huge teams that disciple thousands, and they understand that they are coaches. They desire that their disciples grow to new levels within an accountability and encouragement structure.

Remember the church planter in chapter 8 who made several pages of notes on what he felt a person must know before he could become a leader? Here's what I told him: "This may be a reason why your church hasn't grown. You expect things of your team that Jesus didn't expect of His (like a Bible college degree). If you require your team to know all those things, most of them will never feel good enough to disciple others."

It's been eight years, and he still has only one hundred people in the church—and a new group of guys to train. Those he used to meet with have left because they never got to play or maybe because they felt overwhelmed and unworthy.

Our goal as a church is to give a foundation to our people and to remind them they are lifelong learners. You can only do so much sitting on the bench. We need to train spiritual soldiers to fight spiritual battles alongside us. If we do this effectively, our people will change the world rather than conform to it.

The job of a coach is to create an environment where every person can grow. He knows the game well enough to know what the player needs. He guides the student through the process of becoming a great player and even a great coach. When we win and train up men and women who are able to win and train up others, growth becomes exponential. It becomes more than a church; it becomes a movement.

A Christian is one who loves God and loves others. Ephesians 2:10 tells us that we are God's masterpiece and that God has good works for us to do which He predestined for us before time began. We do not do good works to be saved. We do them *because* we are saved. We are a part of God's team—on a mission to save the world, on a mission to help other believers finish what they started. We are to be ambassadors for Jesus (see 2 Cor. 5).

A WORD OF CAUTION

As we put this plan together, it was never our intention to build a comprehensive process for discipleship. People are so different, as are their needs, backgrounds, and leadership and learning styles. Our goal was to try to put together a process that would give people a place to start. Our heart is to see people discipled. Once people are won to the Lord, they must be given the tools they will need to become mature in Christ and to battle against our enemy, the devil.

In any man-made process there are weaknesses and holes. This model is truly incomplete, and many of you may already be thinking of things you would change. We wanted you to think about the discipleship process—what it is, how it works, and how to implement it. At Real Life, we adapt it to the different leaders and groups we have.

I also know that some will use what we have created in a way that was not intended by us. Understand *our* heart in this: we want to help our people mature in Christ. At Real Life we are not legalist about using this process. It is a guide, a tool, not a set of laws that must be followed. The Word alone is our guidebook. It would grieve us if people understand this process better than they understand the Word of God. It is our desire that God will be glorified in what we have attempted to do.

As in anything that is subject to human nature, there will be some who will place values on themselves and others based on where they are in the process: "I am a Ministry-level person and you are only a Connect-level person." Understand that these categories are only stages of development. To say one is better than another would be as foolish as saying a junior in high school is better than a sophomore. They are of equal value; they are just in different places in the process.

Others will be hard on themselves, believing they cannot move past the Connect level because they struggle with their motives. To be honest, we all fall into the self-centered "me" thinking at times. We all struggle to be other-centered, mature followers of Christ.

I want to emphasize that a good, healthy discipleship program does not endow its leaders with authoritarian control over their groups. I believe very much in discipleship, but over the years several groups have emerged with teachings that the discipleship leaders were somehow above questioning. Spiritual abuse is possible in any relationship. We do not want to see people believing that God speaks through their leader in a cultish way. We want Disciple-level people to act as a guide and friend. No one is above being wrong or being questioned. The Word is our guide, and the Holy Spirit will speak if someone starts to become spiritually abusive.

We also have a home group structure designed to make sure there is accountability. By accountability, I mean the small group leaders will be held accountable as to how they lead. Community pastors and coaches are there to make sure that the Lord is being honored in all we do. Remember, the job of the Disciple-level person is to raise up and release people, not control them. Our leaders give advice but have no power to command. We want people to have right theology and right action, but there is freedom in Christ, not bondage.

May our process be a vehicle to help form winning teams for many churches.

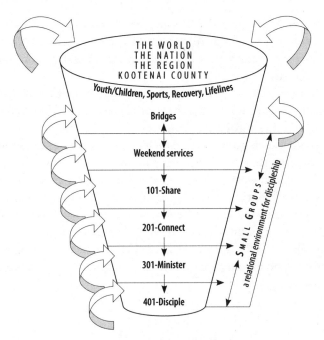

"Reaching the Whole World for Jesus, One Person at a Time!"
Acts 1:8 "But when the Holy Spirit has come upon you, you will receive power and will tell people about me everywhere—in Jerusalem, throughout Judea, in Samaria, and to the ends of the earth."

THE FUNNEL CHART

Our church has put together this chart that attempts to lay out our entire strategy for others to see and understand.

The 101 (Share Level) Class teaches them what we believe about salvation, basic theology, church structure, and philosophy.

The 201 (Connect Level) Class gets them connected if they are not already. It teaches them the basics of discipleship, what a disciple is, and where they are in the discipleship process.

The 301 (Ministry Level) Class explains what a leader in our church is expected to do. The job description and expectations of a leader are clearly explained. We have all our leaders go through the 301 every year.

The 401 (Disciple Level) Class teaches ministry skill sets to our leaders as well as deeper spiritual and theological truths. As we discover weaknesses, we create new classes that we add to the 401 Class list.

Every road leads to a small group where our people learn to actually live out the truths that our classes teach. They become small churches within the church.

As our leaders grow and find their position on the team through this process, they are moved back up into the system. Some will become youth workers, some small group leaders, and some will help us reach out to the world through our local sports programs, recovery ministry, etc. Others will become church planters in the region or country and still others will become missionaries somewhere else in the world. Every believer will have a place to minister, and all our disciples should become disciple makers at some level.

11

PUTTING THE ROOKIE IN

Turning Players Loose

In the early years at Real Life, we faced several problems. We were growing so quickly that we had to put people into small group leadership even though they had not been discipled adequately. We had people who had been Christians for some time, but they had come from churches that had not allowed or encouraged them to grow into leadership positions. They had sat in the show for years but had no working experience in discipling others. To be honest, I wouldn't change much about how we handled it. It was messy, but ministry often is. Our people had to grow up quickly. We were a bunch of rookies learning together. The truth is, we have to stop being afraid to put the rookies in the game. The benefits far outweigh the problems.

ROOKIES NEED ACCOUNTABILITY

In those early groups, we did "on-the-job training" with those who were willing. We had to trust the Lord to guide and protect our church as we developed a reproducible process to train leaders.

You might say that sounds dangerous, as these folks could lead people astray. You're right, but we had to trust the Holy Spirit to help us. We made sure that our small group leaders had effective coaches to provide oversight and accountability, and we also provided curriculum for the groups. Yes, there were times we had to confront a leader in love if he tried to do his own thing. When we did this, more often than not we remained friends and fellow teammates. We had to aggressively and lovingly set the tone. Confrontation, done in the right way, isn't easy, but it is imperative to an effective structure and strategy.

We also knew that the discipleship process went beyond curriculum. There were those who had come from churches where a transfer of information was the only goal. Some who had sat under great teachers sought to imitate them, though they did not have the gift of teaching and did not know how to use the Word properly. We had to show them how to use good curriculum that allowed them to ask good questions and facilitate conversation.

Our new leaders also needed to be taught that their responsibility went beyond the group meeting. Our leaders were to pastor their small groups of people. They were to call the missing, visit the sick, and pray with the hurting. We needed them to create an environment where relationship could be developed. Most of our leaders had not experienced being loved by a pastor, so they did not know how to love someone, or how to pray for the sick since they had never seen it. We had to teach them.

BENEFITS TO GETTING THE ROOKIES IN THE GAME

As I said, the best way to learn is to be in the game under the guidance of a coach (Disciple-level person). You become a great player by playing, first in practice, then in a real game. The job of the coaching staff is to get players into the game. In most churches there are only a few pastors, and if someone in the congregation is having a problem, it's tough to get an appointment with a busy man. There are too few pastors to handle the needs of all the people. Many churches only allow their people to serve in ground-level ways. I don't have a problem with this being the starting point, but God's plan includes making people into fully functional disciples of Jesus.

Have you ever watched a game with someone who gets so into it, he talks to the television? Maybe that's you. I'll admit I've caught myself doing that a time or two. The football team comes to the line of scrimmage, the quarterback barks out the signals, and the ball is snapped. He drops back and scans the field. You stare at the television as the quarterback starts to scramble. You yell, "Throw it to 84! He's open! He's open!" The quarterback is sacked, and your team loses its last chance to tie the game. You're shocked! "What an idiot. He was open," you sigh in disgust.

It doesn't occur to you that maybe the guy couldn't see number 84 was open because he was worried about the three-hundred-pound men chasing him, or that the six-foot-two quarterback might not be able to see over the six-foot-eight defensive tackle. It's easy to criticize those playing when you have no idea what it's like to be on the field in their position.

When people are in the game and not allowed to become pew-sitting critics, they discover it's easy to make a mistake. They come to understand that when you're speaking in front of people, you might get nervous and say something you didn't mean. They know you can do your best and fail. In a church where failure is expected, people extend understanding and grace.

I remember one of the first times I had another guy give a communion meditation in our church. He was nervous and he rambled. He was trying, but he was saying things I know he didn't believe, like the bread was the actual body of Jesus rather than the bread represented his body. Some of our older members were freaked.

After he was done, I got up to preach and started off by saying, "Wasn't John great? This was the first time he's given the communion meditation, and I know he was nervous. Some of you have been Christians for a long time, and we're going to need you to help us in areas you might have no experience in. We want to provide opportunities for you to learn while stepping outside your comfort zone." When people have had the experience of playing on the field and tried but failed, they really do become grace givers rather than critics. By the same token, if the only position you give a person is that of a critic (watcher), don't get mad at them when they do the only thing they are allowed to do: criticize.

Becoming Personally Vested

Discipleship produces people who care about their teammates, the coaches, the equipment, the plays, the field, and about whether the team is winning!

When I played high school football, we were in the semifinals of the state playoffs. We were down 20–16 with about a minute left in the game. We blocked a punt and were driving down the field to score. As the quarterback, I threw the ball to our wide receiver across the middle, and he ran to the other team's 40. On the next play, I threw the ball to my tight end at the 20. He had a great game! We called a time-out with twenty-two seconds left and set up the perfect play. Everyone would go to the corners, except our tight end who would sneak underneath the coverage after faking a block. I would hit him to get us close to the goal line and then call a time-out. After using this last time-out, we would have at least two chances to get into the end zone and win.

I dropped back. It worked perfectly; my tight end released, and I hit him in the numbers. I will never forget how he turned on the speed to the end zone. There was no way anyone would stop him. He was open all the way, but then, at the last second, a player appeared out of nowhere. I remember throwing my arms in the air, believing it wouldn't matter, because our player was a big boy.

I knew he could walk right over the top of the defensive back. But something happened and on the 1-yard line he dropped the ball. There was a mad dash, but it was too late. With five seconds left in the game, we lost the ball as well as our chance at the state championship.

I was devastated. The guy who lost the ball was devastated. The other team ran out the clock, and there we stood, heartbroken, our dreams shattered. My friend, the tight end, knelt crying. He was a broken young man, crushed by the loss and feeling like he had ruined it for us all. I must admit that though I patted him on the shoulder, I was upset. I was not the friend I should have been. I wanted to help him and kill him at the same time.

As we walked back to the locker room, some of my teammates came running over, laughing and shoving each other. They wanted to know where we were going for pizza. I wanted to smack them! But then I realized they were the guys who never got to play. They were the ones who sat on the bench, along for the ride. Sure, they were bummed not to get another weekday off of school, but it occurred to me: those on the bench have little at stake in how the team does. Their heart and soul are not as involved; they are spectators in uniforms.

This is a major problem in many churches. It's why people bounce around from church to church. There's nothing at stake for them. They stay in one place as long as no one offends them, or until the sermon series they like is over, or as long as they like the music. They don't care when the team loses because it wasn't something they invested in, and I don't mean just financially. They don't participate in any ministry; they haven't invested their personal time physically or emotionally. They have put forth no effort caring for others. They have nothing at stake!

When people stay on the bench, they don't get the opportunity to become good players; they don't get the chance to invest. They are able to play it safe. What a shame. They miss out on it all—the challenges, the relationships, the blessings, and the victory.

PART 4

ON THE OFFENSIVE

READING FROM
THE SAME PLAYBOOK

How to Align Your Team for Victory

Imagine Joe has just become the coach of his favorite NFL team. Preseason training is just beginning, and Joe has decided that he will wait outside to meet the players as they drive up to the complex. He is excited to meet them. With all the talent Joe has been blessed with this season, he knows that this year he can win!

As Joe is waiting, the first limo pulls up, and his star quarterback gets out of the car. He strolls up to Joe with a big smile and says, "Coach, nice to meet you. I know you are glad to meet me too, and I know that you understand the value I bring to the team. I am without a doubt the most important person on this team, and I have put together a playbook accentuating my outstanding qualities. If this team is to win, and I am to participate, you will need to run the list of plays that I have created."

Joe smiles and says thank you just as the next limo pulls up. His star tailback gets out, approaches, and gives Joe a big hug. He says, "I know I was just traded to this team, but I am confident you understand what outstanding possibilities I bring. I have put together this playbook that will enable us to win because it is designed to use me at my full potential. If you know what is best for the team, you will run by this playbook!"

Within hours, player after player comes with his own playbook, each uniquely designed according to the specific skills of their authors, all designed to make *them* the star. At the end of the day, Joe has a hundred playbooks. How can he make everyone happy? How can his team work together when each player believes *he* is the most important player and the team should revolve around him? He can't! Would any coach with half a brain even try?

This is often how many churches deal with their people. Many of God's coaches have no playbook to give the potential players that may come to their teams. They let people do what they want or, just as bad, they let them do nothing, just sit and watch the coach perform. As a result, these players will unintentionally make a mess of the plays called by the coaches or they will come up with their own playbook and entice others to follow it. It's trouble either way.

The job of the coach (the minister) is to say, "We already have a playbook, one given to us by God. We have a system on this team that has been developed by the leaders who are listening to the Lord. If you want to be on this team, we will all play by the same playbook that everyone else on this team plays by—the plan designed to allow us to win *together*."

IT STARTS WITH THE COACHING STAFF

When we first started conferences at Real Life, we thought that the reason most churches failed was their methodology. We found instead that the first problem was a lack of unity in the leadership. We kept in mind a horror story we had heard following a Christian conference put on by another church. A pastor who had attended was inspired to implement change at his church, and he went home and immediately began some of the suggested changes. A war started because the rest of the leadership, who had not been at the conference, were not convinced and did not see the need for the changes. As a result, the church imploded and all possibility of positive change was lost for several years. We knew our team needed to do it differently. In the conferences that we have organized, we only allow churches to come that are willing to bring their entire staff or board so they can learn the lessons together. They must decide together what they will do on the team God gave them to lead.

FROM THE STAFF TO THE PLAYERS

Once the leadership is on the same page, it is essential that you put together an official playbook all the players can read and understand. In our church it is the 101–201–301–401 classes. We took the names from Saddleback Church in California and changed the content to fit who we are. Classes alone won't get everyone on the same page, so we also write small group curriculum, preach sermons, and have team trainings that share the vision with our people.

It takes practice for a team to be able to call a play and have everyone know their part. It takes work. It takes accountability. It takes acceptance from all the major players in your church. It takes time. Most importantly, it takes repetition.

We often ask ourselves in team meetings, "How many times do we have to say this?" Remember, you are dealing with people who are not on the inside. If you have said it a hundred times, maybe they have heard it only ten times. You will have a constant influx of new players coming in at Easter, at weekly services, or through your small groups who have never heard it. For a culture to be created, you must speak it over and over—live it and breathe it.

In pro sports there are new draft picks every year. Players are traded, and free agents move from team to team. When players join a new team, they must learn the team's system. Can you imagine if they didn't? It would be chaos! They'd be running over each other. There can only be one playbook, one system. A team that will not work together will never win.

Church life is the same. If the leadership of a church has agreed upon a system but cannot get the players to run by the plan, that team cannot win. People choose a church based primarily on the one that meets their needs. They come with expectations and demands. Many have come from other churches that ran a different system or no system at all. They may not bring you their playbook, but they definitely run by their own set of understandings and expectations.

It's difficult to get Christians to work together. There are many excellent Bible teachers on the radio and many good books written by great pastors. Each offers a different successful system or plan. Some Christians listen to a coach on the radio five times a week but only hear their pastor two or three times a month. When multiple coaches are pointing in contradictory directions, you have a mess on your hands. If the church leadership doesn't understand the dilemma and take appropriate action by communicating effectively, it's possible for people to know what is happening at other successful churches but not know the game plan for their own team.

Once again, the leadership must intentionally bring the team together. A good coach must have a way to bring the new players on board and keep the existing players inspired—all going the same direction. There must be a common language, a common goal. The struggle for a team that has never won is to get them to act like a team that can. The biggest struggle for a team that won last year is to get them *together* again to win this year. Even those who may have done it once often fail to understand the important dynamics of *continuing in the fundamentals year after year.*

FOCUSING THE TEAM WITH CLASSES

At RLM we use classes to teach the concepts. Our goal is for those who want to join our team to understand what we are about.

Yes, in these classes we do seek to transfer information. But the small groups and ministries also become the place where these principles (the information) are lived out in practice. We start with a Joining the Team class that is offered every month. Our 101 class is designed as an overview of our playbook. We share with our new people the "state of the church in America," and most are blown away by the fact that even with the truth, the church in America is failing in its mission. We share with them the importance of working together as one. In 1 Corinthians 1:10, Paul encourages the team to work together: "I appeal to you, brothers, in the name of our Lord Jesus Christ, that all of you agree with one another so that there may be no divisions among you and that you may be perfectly united in mind and thought."

We share with them that Jesus also tells His future team that the message will not be delivered powerfully or effectively if the team will not work together (see John 17). We talk about what makes a team, and illustrate the huge task that we face by asking those in the class (usually about 100), to share their church background. By the end of this share session, we generally find about fourteen denominational backgrounds represented. We ask the group at this point, "Can you see a potential problem?" The answer is an obvious yes.

We point out that unless we at RLM get on the same page, we would be like many churches in America; we would lose. We then present how the RLM team works and where we are going, and we end with an invitation to join the team. If they are not interested in leaving their personal agendas and past playbooks behind, we encourage them to look for another team. We tell them, "At Real Life, *people must agree to this playbook and our unique execution of the plays if they want to be involved on the field with this team.*" They must sign a covenant and agree to the code of conduct given to us by God in his ultimate playbook, the Bible.

This Joining the Team class has saved us much grief over the years. We are able to lovingly confront people who wander away from the playbook and help them understand again what they are doing. We have been able to bring in new people with a common understanding and commitment. This class has been effective because it also works as a filter to keep out those who would not agree to the team's goals, methods, and biblical principles.

Sometimes in churches we are desperate to find volunteers, so we look for any well-groomed, warm body who is able to use the right language and seems to have an understanding of ministry. Only after they are on the field do we find out we have a problem with semantics. They use the same words, but their real message and agenda are different and contrary to our team playbook. They can really mess up the play in the game. When we have to take them out of the game, it's painful because they may have already built relationships that give them the ability (on purpose or not) to mislead groups of individuals. Sometimes this can lead to factions and even a church split.

After our people attend the 101 class, the next step is the 201 class. This class explains the discipleship process to people who more than likely have not understood what a disciple is. Most American Christians have little understanding of the Word. We explain the different levels (Share, Connect, Ministry, Disciple) and show them where they are in the process and where they need to go next to grow. We open the door to connection groups if they are not already in a small group, and we start the process of helping them understand their gifting and talents and how they can be used for ministry.

At Real Life, every leader including myself, our staff, and our elders must take our 301 (Ministry-level) class every year. Our new leaders will take it as they take on leadership responsibility, and our existing leadership is brought back to the fundamentals of our team by repeating the class yearly. They are also reminded of the essential doctrine of our church and of the way we will respond to non-salvation issues within our ministries. They again sign the 301 covenant, which outlines what it means to be a leader in our church, and they recommit to practicing these fundamentals.

The goal is not to come up with something new but to commit to the things that have made us a winning church. Can you imagine a coach telling his team that those who knew the playbook from last year would be exempt from studying it this year? Every year a good coach takes his team through the fundamentals again.

If your church is like ours, some of your people grew up on other teams. We are not naïve enough to believe that one class will undo all of the habits and beliefs people hold. Couple that with pastors they listen to on the radio weekly, along with the Christian books they read, and the Christian TV programs they watch, we realize it is a huge job to make sure that our leaders stay on course. Every year we must remind them of where we stand and where we are going.

By now I am sure you realize we believe that a pastor's job—the coach's job—is to raise up people to do what we do. At Real Life we take our leaders through ongoing training, our 401 (Disciple-level) classes. Our goal is to continue their education by teaching skill sets they will need to pastor and lead their individual groups. These classes may teach them to defend the Scriptures, help them learn to facilitate a group more effectively, train them in entry-level counseling, or cover things like hospital visitation. We usually offer classes in a classroom setting, but we also offer them on DVDs, on CDs, or through the Internet. We want our people to learn the material or skills at a time that is convenient for them. We want them to have enough time to do their regular job, take care of their family, and still be able to minister. We have found that our leaders love to listen to the CDs while commuting. They get to learn without taking time away from their family or ministry. We want our people to have their life in balance.

CONSTANT VISION CASTING

Repetition is the key to learning. We have heard that a person needs to hear something 1,000 to 10,000 times before they make it their own. Obviously, classes alone are not enough. One of the other things we do is preach a series on RLM's goals every year. The goals are then taught in our small groups with curriculum that corresponds with the sermon series.

Every week I remind those who come how important it is to be connected in a small group. It is the place we get pastored and discipled. We also show a video of the previous week's baptisms in each service. It's one more way we remind our people why we exist: to reach the world for Jesus.

Many come to North Idaho to get away from people, as I did. In a big church it can be uncomfortable. I often remind people why we have to wait in lines to check our kids into the children's programs, why we walk a quarter of a mile from a parking spot to the front doors. It is not about our comfort, obviously. Jesus became entirely uncomfortable to save us, and now we get to join Him in His mission to save the world. It is a privilege for us to be a part of something great.

TEAM HUDDLES

We further reinforce our vision through leadership huddles that we call Focus Events. For those who have been leaders on the team, we have these vision casting events twice each year. We share all that God has done since the last time we met together—the number of decisions for Christ that have been made, how many small groups have been started, the number of new leaders that are ministering, and the new ministries that have been started. We show a video with all of the baptisms from the previous six months. It's moving to watch our people applaud and cry as they see what God is doing.

Keeping relationships with our leaders is of utmost importance. Sharing our hearts with them is one of the best ways we know to avoid problems and mistrust. We know the devil is working overtime to cause them to doubt us and divide God's team, so we want to meet him head on and share who we are on a regular basis.

We wrap up by giving God the glory for the great work He has done. We praise our leaders for working together, for serving and giving. We also share our struggles and ask them to pray with us about decisions that need to be made. Sometimes we show our appreciation by giving them a gift, bringing in a comedian, or hosting a BBQ. By the end of these times, our people are fired up and feel a part of what is happening.

To further honor and inform our leaders, I send out a leadership email that shares upcoming events and points of interest. They have earned the right to know before anyone else because of their service. It does not show respect to your leaders if they find out important information at the same time as those who just attend. When we are praying about decisions that will affect our leaders, we send them information and ask them to pray and respond.

You can have all the talent in the world, but if you cannot get and keep your team running the same play at the same time, you'll lose. Recently we had leaders come in from a fast-growing church. I did what I always do. I let them talk to whomever they wanted. Brandon, our small groups pastor, got them into meetings with our staff and volunteers for two days straight. At the end of the time I sat down with them. I knew they had questions for me, but I also had questions for them. I wanted to know what they found. I wanted to see if our team (staff and volunteers) was sharing a consistent vision with consistent language. I wanted to see if what we believe was being passed through the staff to the leaders to the people sitting in the chairs.

They were excited as they told me that RLM is all about team, relationship, and discipleship. They got solemn as they expressed that their church, though it was growing, was disconnected. The staff did not work as a team; everyone did their own thing. I asked them what the philosophy and vision of their church was. They thought for a minute and said, "I guess we don't really have one. We don't have a common language or a set direction." When I asked what they thought I would think their philosophy was if I came and watched and talked to their people, the executive pastor said, "Well, I think the unstated goal of the church is to have everyone come and listen to our pastor talk." How sad!

The job of a leadership team in a church is to guide the team to a God-glorifying, biblical vision. The job of a coaching staff is to make sure that everyone is running the same play at the same time and that everyone knows the goal of the team and is able to state the goals effectively.

13

CHURCH IS
A TEAM SPORT

Creating a Culture of Teamwork

God wants His team to work together for His glory. Teamwork is essential to winning, and I believe that church really is a team sport. Each believer has a function that is essential to the success of the mission. We must be unified to win, just as a team of talented individuals cannot win without teamwork. Coaches are in charge of the training process, and the individual must come second to the team and the cause.

It sounds simple, but there's a problem. We have an enemy seeking to push each individual to the top. Pride is the ally of the enemy. Because of pride, the devil rebelled against God. Because of our desire to be like God, we rebelled. Our sinful nature is all about us. We want to chase our own dreams even if it means running over the top of someone else.

177

IT STARTS AT THE TOP

Pride is the pitfall of every good team. Pride will cause division, kill relationships, and tell you that you don't need to work as hard as you once did. There must be humility and sacrifice if a team is to win. Remember, the coach is responsible for keeping pride at a minimum on his team. It starts with the coach who then must build a climate of humility, cooperation, and teamwork.

If a coach isn't careful, he can circumvent his own philosophy by the way he acts. He may want his people to function as a team but not be willing to lead that way himself. He becomes the dictator, the one with all the answers, the one who takes credit for the success of the team, who blames others when the team encounters a setback. A good coach models teamwork and expects the other coaches and players to follow and do the same.

In the church world, the pastor is often the one at the top of the food chain. He sits in his position of authority and uses the pulpit to give marching orders. Some create a theology around this kind of thinking. The leader thinks that he alone has God's ear and God's revelation. He then becomes unwilling to allow others to speak into the vision, so the team loses the war from lack of counsel.

People often support this kind of thinking as well. Somehow we humans either refuse to listen to people or we give our minds over to those who would like to lead us because we need someone to follow, even if it is the wrong person. God has gifted leaders to preach, organize, and lead. But we must remember that God does not seek to glorify men; He seeks to be glorified by men. God has given everyone in the church gifts to glorify Him and the ability to help build up the body of Christ. As a team, we will work together to accomplish the purposes of God. If there is a climate or culture of teamwork in the church, it must start at the top.

THE BENEFITS OF JOINT LEADERSHIP

One way to promote a climate of teamwork is to shy away from things that promote the individual. This is why the Lord instituted the kind of leadership He did in the church. God's structure is one of elders (plural) who work together to make decisions. Not only is this biblical, but there are many benefits to this system.

The first is accountability. A leader who has free rein to do what he wishes is in a dangerous situation. Power without accountability corrupts.

Second, many leaders working together can see more than one can alone. Some pastors have elderships where they surround themselves with those who see things the way they do or those who will give in when pushed. This is foolish. Scripture tells us multiple counselors give wisdom. Others are gifted in ways the pastor is not. Ideas might be better created and received when there are multiple perspectives contributing to their creation. It often takes more time to make decisions when going through a group, but there are fewer messes to clean up later. Team leadership creates a value-driven organization instead of a personality-led one.

Third, when the congregation knows there is a team working together for their best interests, it gives them a sense of security, much like a child with two parents who love and respect each other and the child. Multiple leaders provide the church with stability. If something happens to one of the leaders, like the pastor, the church would be able to move forward because multiple leaders have the same accepted vision.

Finally, with a joint leadership team you are promoting what you value by your example. As a leader in our church, I want to be the example and promoter of teamwork in all I do. This happens when I see others' opinions as valid and worthwhile, even when I may disagree. I don't want to throw down the "boss card" with my staff unless someone is going away from the direction God has shown us collectively. If I have done my job of discipling our leaders, and we have established the course together, they are just as capable of knowing what to do as I am.

SERMON CLUB

Every week at RLM, a good portion of the staff meet with me in Sermon Club. We generally work on the sermon a few weeks out. Doing that allows time for our other ministries to find or develop dramas, videos, or props that will help drive the message home.

The most important reason for Sermon Club is that working together with men and women who are involved in ministering to our people brings wisdom. It seems like most pastors believe if they preach better sermons, more people will come. Some spend lots of time praying and studying before they preach; others don't plan at all and spend little time looking through the Scriptures for answers. The latter forget that they have a responsibility to do their best for the Lord, but the former spend too much time preparing for something that provides the least results. These pastors don't have time to be in relationship with their people.

I believe if you spend more time getting to know people, they will listen because they know you love them. When you spend time with people, you won't have to guess what they are going through in order to preach sermons that are relevant to their lives. Sermon Club is my answer to several problems related to preaching.

1. My goal is to prepare disciples who can disciple others. Sermon Club gives my staff, some of whom are future preachers, a chance to see how a sermon is created. They see the technical side along with how verses are put together and understood.

2. Sermon Club is an answer to my sermon preparation problem. How can I create good sermons in less time so that I can spend more time with the flock and have more time to disciple future leaders? In one hour I sit with the staff and am exposed to years of biblical theological education and knowledge about life. They have so many life experiences to share along with great illustrations. I throw out the topic along with a general outline, and they give me more ideas

than I can use. They bring things to light that I may not have thought of.

3. These meetings also give me an opportunity to hear about the cares and concerns of people from the congregation. Our staff has more contact with people than I possibly could have, so I get a broader feel for the congregation's needs.

4. Perhaps one of the most valuable aspects to this method is the varying perspectives. Individuals share what they think would be the best way for me to speak to people in their demographic and ministry groups. Genette, our women's minister, shares how a message can be effective in helping our women. Sandy, who works with single moms, points out when I need to be careful in my application of a point; she reminds me that those who have been hurt don't need condemnation. Nick Smoot and Thad DeBuhr, our youth ministers, help me apply the Word to our youth.

5. A coach must make the team feel valued. These meetings are a great place for me to reinforce to the team that their opinions are important and can make a difference. When you allow your team, whether they are volunteer or paid, to share in the development of what matters most to you, it builds a climate that filters down to everyone. It becomes part of your culture.

6. By the end of Sermon Club, we have created something we worked on together. I've modeled teamwork and I let the congregation know that *we* came up with this message together so they don't give me too much credit. I have something that can apply to every age group. I am training new preachers. Our group knows what I am preaching about so that they can reinforce the message in groups they lead throughout the entire church and be prepared for those who have questions.

This is often the most productive hour of my week.

SHARED PREACHING

In the last year the Lord pushed me further down the road of living out what I believe. As the number of services grew, I found my voice was suffering and my energy level was decreasing. As I would get tired, I did what we all do. I whined. My ability to see what needed to be done and do it at the leadership level was declining. I could not get off the merry-go-round long enough to plan for the future. I felt pressure to preach because our people didn't like it when I didn't. I started to feel like preaching was a burden, and I resented people for putting pressure on me. I felt like I was taking a final exam every week graded by 8,000 people, not including the radio audience.

At the same time, I liked being the only guy they wanted to hear. I liked being told that I was anointed by God to speak. I loved and hated preaching at the same time. As I spent time with the Lord and with wise counsel, I realized I was walking a path that was dangerous for me. I liked the glory. I hated the pressure. I was tired spiritually.

I was in the office working on the next sermon series, tired as usual, when one of my close friends and staff members came in to see how I was doing. I told him I was tired, and he asked if he could share something with me. He said some things I didn't really want to hear. He shared that I was not living out my own philosophy when it came to preaching. He asked why I wasn't raising up people to do what I was doing. He told me I was losing my joy, and I was at risk for burnout. I did not like what he said, but it brought to mind the concerns of our elders who had mentioned this to me some weeks before.

I believed in the philosophy of raising people up, but my actions weren't reflecting it. I needed to live what I believe. I realized at that moment that I believed something I wasn't doing and that forced me to the edge. My thoughts turned to the question, "Am I willing to do that?" I wrote down a new commitment in my journal. I knew God was trying to get through my thick skull, and it was time to listen.

I decided to make some changes. I went to my staff and asked some of them to start team teaching with me. I knew the congregation was used to hearing me. Rather than just making a transition to having someone preach in my stead, I started sharing time with them. My plan was to share time with someone for a while, then to let them preach without me. By doing this it would allow our church family time to get used to others speaking.

This accomplished several goals: the congregation got used to hearing another perspective, and they saw that I approved of the person speaking with me; it saved my voice; it allowed others to see that these guys could answer questions and pastor them as well as I could; and it allowed my staff the opportunity to speak in front of large crowds. But most importantly, I was being consistent with my philosophy. I moved from theory into practice. I was being a good coach.

14

WHEN THE GOING
GETS TOUGH

Getting Real with Each Other

When we started training leadership from other churches, we thought we'd find the biggest need would be new methodology. We were wrong. The greatest need was for unity.

Over the years, I have seen too many battles between elders, boards, and staff. Some had unresolved issues; others could not and did not want to work together. Some actually thought they could serve God effectively while undercutting and backbiting and carrying around hurt, resentment, and bitterness.

Some elders and staff have allowed upset congregants, and even staff members, to bypass God's plan of reconciliation as outlined in Matthew 18. As a result, the sun has gone down on their anger and the devil now has a foothold in their churches, causing division and a lack of effectiveness. I have seen full-scale battles because the leadership couldn't agree on what winning looked like or how to accomplish it. It may seem to be a battle about direction, but that is usually a cover for personality issues and unresolved conflict. These battles over hurt feelings and opinions give me flashbacks to the movie *Braveheart*, when William Wallace asked the clans to unite, but all they would do was squabble. They had the ability to take their country back from the British tyrant Longshanks, but they didn't.

The job of the leader is to unite the clans, the team members. A good coach unites his team leaders with a common vision, but he also must bring his team together into a relationship that resembles godly, loving, nurturing, Christian fellowship. Relationships are like ropes that tie people together. The more ropes, the more stable you'll be on the side of the mountain you are climbing.

In my high school and college days, we knew as a team we were going to win if we could frustrate the opposing players enough to cause them to fight in their huddle. If we could get them to blame each other or resent the other players on their team, we were already halfway to victory. Satan knows this tactic well. Bickering among team leadership or staff will destroy a team.

The Most Important Component

The church works when God blesses it. Remember, it is God who makes the church grow (see Acts 2:47; 1 Cor. 3). A house divided against itself cannot stand (see Matt. 12:25). Jesus tells us that when you know your brother has something against you, you must go and make it right, and then come back and give your sacrifice (see Matt. 5:23). When there is strife between brothers, God won't accept a sacrifice, let alone bless the church. How can we expect to win or go forward if God isn't blessing us?

The coach has to create an environment and an expectation of forgiveness, humility, and cooperation. He has to promote a vision of what could be, by making sure the church is what it should be. We will never achieve a positive future if we can't be who we need to be right now. A good coach encourages others to forgive not only because we are called to but for the sake of the cause of Christ. It is the only way we can win. If we are who we are supposed to be, the rest will fall into line and take care of itself.

THE WORLD NEEDS A MODEL

Many things are at stake when it comes to the battle to be in relationship. First, we live in a world that knows it is in need of love. We were created with a need to be in relationship with God and with other people. Because of sin, separation from God transpired, which led immediately to broken relationships with people. Eventually, God said it grieved Him to have even made man (see Gen. 6:6). Our sinful nature led to a broken, dark, lonely world. In the darkness, people stumble over each other as they selfishly fight to get what they think they need or want.

Jesus came to pay for our sins, but He also came to restore relationships. The power that is supplied by the Holy Spirit enables us to love the way God intended. The church, the way God designed it, was to be a real working family, amongst families that had failed. The church was to be a light to show the world what real love looked like. It would glorify God by being an example of what God could do. If the world could see God's kind of relationships in the church, they would come looking for what we have.

God's plan was to draw the world to Himself through the greatest love act the world had ever seen. His team has been given the job of delivering the same message through acts of love to a world badly in need of them. As pastors we have often preached the message with our mouths but not with our hearts and actions. As disciples, our job is not only to transfer information about the definition of love but also to model love in our actions. People need living models of what love looks like.

Our staff and leadership positions come with a responsibility to model relationship so our emerging disciples can see it. Creating a culture takes more than just coming up with a new, pithy language upon which we all can agree. It is not just coming up with a strategy that seems biblical. To create a culture, we must be living models of what it looks like to love. To stay in relationships is hard work; it is a spiritual battle we face. We are fighting to connect people to God, and we are in a war to keep our team together.

If Christian leaders, supposedly committed to Jesus and to His ways, empowered by the Holy Spirit, cannot stay in relationships, then what hope do our new believers have? What reason would the world have for wanting to come with us anywhere? If all we offer are broken relationships, seasoned with a little guilt, why would they want what we have?

God's Leaders Need Encouragement

Encouragement is another reason relationships are a must for God's leaders. We are in a spiritual fight. This last year was perhaps the hardest of my ministry career. I hit a wall. The church had grown again, and we were getting ready to do another building campaign. I had preached five times a weekend for fifty of the fifty-two weeks. (Yes, I know it was stupid.) Then one of our elders, a very close friend, was diagnosed with terminal cancer. We were also in the spotlight in our area and were under attack from the enemy who was using some very unkind people disguised as Christians. My oldest son was struggling, as was my wife, and I did not know what to do. I had worked too hard for too many hours, and I was burnt out. I started to question my calling. I started to struggle with my faith. I became a negative person, and it was affecting my whole life. Even hunting, something I normally loved to do, sounded tiring.

If it had not been for some close relationships in my life, I would not have made it through those very dark months. Not only was my wife a rock and my parents supportive, the ministry staff and elders stepped up as real friends to help me get through. They noticed the changes and began to talk with me about how I was feeling. They prayed for me. They stepped in to help me with my son, instead of judging me. They didn't expect me to be perfect. They let me vent my frustration with God. They also told me the truth, though it wasn't always easy to hear. I had real friends who walked with me through the "valley of the shadow of death." I'm not sure where I'd be had it not been for those relationships.

In those first churches where I served, I had been alone for the most part. Oh, I had a few friends, but these churches did not provide relational environments. Most people did their own thing, never sharing difficulties, doubts, or fears. I remember wishing that I could have friends like the apostle Paul, as he went about on his travels. Oh, to be on a team with people in ministry the same way I have been on a team in sports. A team where people understood each other and looked past each other's faults. People I could trust with my life and my wife. Now I finally had that in the church. Man, it felt good!

One of the things that bothers me when dealing with other churches is that I often see in them now what I saw in my own churches before I came to Real Life. I see staff who are alone, trying their best, but not trusting those they work with enough to open up; senior pastors who think they have to be perfect, the answer man, always joyful, and always filled with faith; people in the church who expect the pastor to be more than human. Pastors are often expected to be people who have already arrived instead of fellow travelers. Many times the congregation does not feel that way, but somehow the pastor believes they do.

I see pastors who are ordinary, fallible people keeping everyone at arm's length because they are afraid. They are afraid if they let people get close, their humanity will be found out, faults and all. Over the years I have heard of many cases where a pastor in need of marital help refused to go because he was afraid people would see him coming out of the counselor's office.

These fears cause people to live in the dark. The devil loves the dark because he can play with our minds there. How many pastors have been caught with secret addictions because they never sought help for fear people would find out? How many join pastors' prayer groups and ministerial associations because they believe that only another senior pastor can understand them? I love working with other pastors and churches, and we ought to work and pray together, but we should also have people on our teams with whom we are honest. We should have friendships—real friendships.

God expects His coaches to create a culture of teamwork and relationship. We must create a culture in our church where it is okay not to be okay. How sad to be in a church where we put on our happy faces and tell everyone that we are fine when we aren't. We live in a world that does not know how to have real relationships; we need to show the world it's okay to struggle, okay to ask for prayer, okay to be sad.

Relationships are hard work. Whether in a marriage, in a parent-child relationship, in a work environment, or in church, it is hard work. In some ways it might be easier to be alone. Many have taken that path. I believe the spiritual war God is fighting is a war over relationship, and if it is, then it is one the Christian soldier must fight as well. The scriptural benefits of these relationships we are committed to are great. We will have support, wisdom, encouragement, spiritual healing, effectiveness, warmth, all of which are too important to miss.

FOCUSING ON THE FUNDAMENTALS

The Importance of Uncluttered Christianity

As I wrote earlier, there was a time when I was disillusioned with the church. I left my childhood home rebellious, looking for any excuse to never darken the door of a church again. The excuse was given to me in college.

My sociology teacher told me Christianity was responsible for the Inquisition, the Crusades, and many other evils in the world. Biology taught me that I was the product of a natural process of evolution. Philosophy taught me there were many roads to heaven, and it was my choice, because I was the ultimate decider of truth. I came away believing God was a crutch for broken people, and since I wasn't broken, I didn't need Him, if He existed at all.

Now remember, my dad was a pastor, so none of this sat too well with him. I recall the day I informed him there was no God. Shocked, he asked, "How did you come up with that?"

I shared my newfound theory. "Real scholars and intellects know the truth about the Bible. It's just one of the myths in the world. You are a Christian because you were brought up Christian. In the same way, Muslims are Muslims because they were brought up Muslim. Buddhists are Buddhists because that was their upbringing. They're all following one myth or another. Evolution proves that there is no need for God, so I think you are all silly."

I will never forget what he said. "Son, you are not an intellectual. What you are saying is foolish. An intellectual is one who studies both sides of the issue, then makes an informed decision. You have not studied the claims you have just made. You're merely quoting other men who have not studied the claims that someone else made to them."

I emphatically reminded him, "I was brought up Christian. I know exactly what people believed and why."

My dad asked, "Why do we believe what we believe?"

I replied, "You have blind, ignorant faith—there is no fact."

"Wrong! I believe the evidence," he said.

"What evidence?" I asked.

He answered, "Your assertion that evolution proves there's no need for God is false. You need to study both sides of the argument. Seek out those who are not evolutionists and ask why they are not. You will discover evolution is a theory not everyone buys into. There are many non-Christian scientists who do not agree with the evolutionary theory. Even many of those who are evolutionists still believe God created the universe through the process of evolution."

After some study, I found out he was right. There were many who had abandoned their own beliefs in evolution after further research. I was still not willing to accept my father's truth, but I was losing some of my confidence in what I would find if I continued the search. My father kept pressing. He knew I was a history major and had always been interested in the past. He sent me the book

Evidence That Demands a Verdict by Josh McDowell. He explained that Josh McDowell had become a Christian by researching Christianity from a historical perspective.

I was in college studying to become a history teacher, so I understood the language and premise of the book my father had sent me. However, I told my dad, "I don't have time to read another book. I'm wrestling, I have classes to take, homework to finish, and a social life to keep up with."

My father replied, "Jim, you are a coward. You have made some big claims. Back them up! If you study this subject and find I am wrong, fine. I will accept that and respect you for doing the research. But if you do not study, I will think you are afraid."

I reluctantly and grudgingly agreed to do the research.

SEEKING TRUTH

I studied many religions, including Buddhism, Islam, Mormonism, and Baha'i. My questions: Is there a true religion? Is there a historically verifiable book that can be trusted to give an accurate story of a religious leader's life and teaching? Is it possible that one of these teachers could lead us to the real God?

I started with Buddhism because I liked the doctrine it espoused. I liked the idea of being God and the idea that there was no hell. However, I found that there was no way to verify any part of the story historically. After studying many of these religions and arriving at the same conclusion, I reluctantly began examining Christianity. I had put it off because I didn't want to believe it could be true. To make a long story short, after several months of study, I came to believe that Christianity is the only historically provable religion.

WILL THE REAL CHRISTIANITY PLEASE STAND UP?

You might think my journey was over, but it wasn't. When I came to the decision that Christianity was true, there was no Promise

Keepers, no Women of Faith, nothing that created some sense of unity between different Christian groups. Back then, there seemed to be no unity among Christians. I had another question: Which Christianity is the real Christianity? The Catholics said that I had to be a Catholic. The Baptists said that if I wasn't a Baptist, I was in trouble. It wasn't enough that I belonged to Jesus, I also needed to belong to the right church, and there seemed to be a lot riding on that decision.

I decided to choose my church in the same way I chose my faith. (Now I know God chose me.) I studied history. I looked at Luther and Calvin, at Wesley, at the rise of the Catholic Church and the Council of Nicea and Trent. I looked at the development of a church, its theology, and historical context. I decided to read the Bible using proper rules for interpretation, starting in Acts to see how the early church practiced their faith. I looked at what they *did* in response to what they believed. I read the Apostolic Fathers, those who were not disciples and not inspired, but were followers of the disciples. They were close enough to the events that they might have some insight. The closer a witness is to the actual event, the better the perspective.

After my study I planned to join the church that had kept the theology and practices of the first church. I would look for a church that stuck to the basics. I understood people had differing views on almost everything, but most Christians had some similar beliefs about essential things, like Jesus is God's Son, the Trinity, salvation by grace through faith, the infallibility of the Bible, the reality of heaven and a hell, and the future return of Jesus to judge the world. It seemed to me that much of what the church argued about had little to do with salvation.

Unity mattered to me. One of the arguments I would use on Christians before I became one was, "You people can't even get along with each other. If Jesus said He came to bring peace, then He must be a liar." Non-Christians notice church splits, angry words, and denominational differences. I used to say, "If Jesus can't keep His word down here, how can I believe He has something better after I die?" After I had worked through my issues with the church,

I wanted to find a church that stood for truth, yet allowed people to disagree, in love, on non-salvation issues.

My Formal Training Years

God eventually directed me to youth ministry, which I did for a few years before I enrolled in Bible college. I'm glad I did. I needed the foundation. However, though I learned many valuable things, many of the classes I took were designed to show how Christians from other denominations were wrong, and the bent of the college was right. For a time, I was the man I had hated in my heathen years in a secular college, ready and willing to fight over everything. I would say that I was fighting for truth and every truth was worth fighting for. For me, it was clear—if they didn't agree, they must have been trying to change the gospel. I judged their motives and their heart.

As I left the Bible college and got into the real world, I found people who truly loved the Lord but had different views on issues that I had formulated opinions on. I also realized that they too had biblical answers to the questions that had been posed in the college classroom. Though I may disagree with their conclusions, they obviously loved the Lord and wanted to serve Him. Typically, we agreed on far more than we disagreed about. I realized that to get something done we had to decide what was a nonnegotiable issue and what was a negotiable issue. I realized that on some issues, greater minds than mine had disagreed for years. I came to the conclusion that not all truth is essential truth. And unity is more important. From this early beginning of my faith, all the way through my formal training, my philosophy for uncluttered Christianity was born and developed.

Avoiding Nonessential Divisive Theology

Let me give you an example of how theology can be divisive. The Scriptures tell us that we are to be baptized. Often the debate has not been about doing it, but *why* you must do it. The Church of Christ emphasizes Acts 2:38. They tell us that baptism is for the remission of sins, so you will receive the gift of the Spirit. They teach that baptism is essential for salvation since you receive the Spirit afterward, and you receive forgiveness through it. Baptists would say that baptism is an outward sign of an inward change. Salvation comes by grace through faith and faith only. You are baptized to become part of the body of Christ: the church. It is an absolute command that is to be obeyed, but not for salvation. I am not here to argue any particular side, though I have my opinions. All the sides believe you must be baptized in water. They agree disciples must baptize because they have been sent by Jesus to do so. However, they disagree on the reasons for and, in some cases, the mode of baptism. Countless fights have taken place over this issue throughout the centuries—usually because someone attached salvation to the discussion. In other words, a teacher claimed that if you do not agree with me you are lost.

Unfortunately, in many cases, Christians fight each other rather than the enemy. Meanwhile, our unsaved neighbors are hurting. They are dying unsaved because we are more consumed with arguing with each other than sharing our faith with them. We fight. They watch. We lose. They lose more.

Uncluttered Christianity says that we do what the Bible says to do, the way the Bible shows us to do it. Yes, in our church we baptize by immersion because we believe that the Scriptures tell us to do so. To baptize means to immerse. That is the definition in the Greek, and was the method of the first church. The disciples did it. All the early fathers did it. The Reformers taught that we should do it. The battle over *why* is answered simply: because the Bible says so. Quit arguing! Zip it! And just do it! Let's get on the same team, give the same message and work together to get some work done for the kingdom!

The goal of our church is to reach the lost with the saving message of Jesus. How can we be a team if we don't give the same message? We share as a body that we are saved by grace, through faith. Faith leads to repentance and confession, baptism, and a life lived for Jesus.

One team, one message, glorifying God by doing what He says
... together.

There are many issues we can highlight that fit into the same
discussion: eternal security, eschatology, the gifts of the Spirit, and
more. Can you be saved, no matter what side of the debate you take
on these issues? If the answer is yes, let's concentrate on things we
can agree on and get the work of the church done.

It is possible to have people who believe in the inerrancy of
Scripture but cannot agree on how to interpret a particular text.
I am not saying there is not an ultimate truth on every subject. I
believe there is. I am just saying that even educated, saved people
can have a different opinion on some of these issues. Again, not
every truth is as important as every other truth.

The goal of Scripture was *not* to get Christians to fight each
other. Jesus promised He would send the Spirit to guide us into
all truth (John 14:15–21; 16:13). Jesus said God would give us
the glory Jesus experienced with the Father: oneness. If Jesus said
these things, made these promises, and meant that we would be
brought to unity on all subjects, there should be less dissension. But
I do not see oneness. I see differing opinions on almost everything.
So maybe there is a different way to look at this. Maybe God has
led us to truth. Not truth on everything, but on the things that
matter most to Him: the Scriptures, the Trinity, and the message
of salvation.

Though we allow differing opinions without judging someone's
salvation, this doesn't mean that as a church we don't set policy for
our people to adhere to as members of the team. In our 101 class,
I make the statement that we will not allow non-salvation issues
to become something that divides the team. I then quote 1 Corinthians 1:10: "I appeal to you, brothers, in the name of our Lord Jesus
Christ, that all of you agree with one another so that there may be
no divisions among you and that you may be perfectly united in
mind and thought." There are truths worth fighting for and there
are truths that should be put aside for the sake of the cause.

Though you can believe different things about non-salvation
issues, the unity and the direction of the church must be preserved.

As coaches, we must have a system that gives every player a place to start and become familiar with our philosophy and stances. It is possible for people to be a part of our team but be listening to other coaches at the same time. We address this in a way that honors coaches who are Bible-believing leaders. We do not treat them as if they are the enemy (unless they are teaching heresy, and even then we do not "fight like the devil" for the things of God). When a different coach teaches something that is not heresy but is different from what we teach, we say, "That is great for that team, but our team has a playbook, and we stick to it so we can be unified."

DEALING WITH DIFFERENCES

I am not saying these non-salvation issues are taboo in our church. We teach that there is a way to discuss these issues that will honor God and others. We also teach our people that there is a time to discuss these things and that they should be careful about who might be around during their discussions. We have many new believers, and we don't want to confuse them or make something more complicated than it needs to be during the early stages of faith.

There is a way to make sure that multiple opinions are respected in your church. As a leader, never give a false picture of another's view or make someone appear to be stupid. Give an accurate, balanced account of both sides. It is best to allow someone you respect, but who differs with you on a subject, to share his or her perspective. Let your people see you disagree as fellow believers. Let them see you honor the other person as you give your account. Let the people see that as Christians, you can disagree on non-salvation issues. When the people on your team see you treat an opposing view with respect, they will do the same.

One of the saddest things I have seen is Christians maligning each other in front of nonbelievers. A few years ago, I experienced one of the most frustrating things I have had to deal with in ministry. A young woman started coming to church. Her marriage was in trouble, and she was ready to hear from the Lord. During a service, she gave her life to Jesus. She started in a small group, and her marriage started to improve. Her countenance changed. But about two months after she gave her life to Jesus, she stopped coming. I immediately started calling to find out what was going on. After many attempts, I got an appointment with her. She was cold and unapproachable.

I asked what had happened. She told me that one of her friends who attended another church told her that our church was a cult because the pastor (that's me) was not a premillennialist. This non-salvation issue had escalated into a scary situation for a young woman who had no idea what was orthodox and what was not.

I called the pastor of that church. Though he was a pastor of a Bible-believing church, he had berated me and other pastors in town for things he deemed important issues. What a shame. This young woman felt like she was in the middle of a war between two people who were supposed to be on the same team. She left both churches for a time.

I believe you should teach truth. You should absolutely teach the things the Bible teaches. For the good of the team, you need to be clear. And you need to be a peacemaker. Spirit-filled Christians should fight only the fights that God wants them to fight. We don't fight because we love to, only because we have to. One fruit of the Spirit is peace. The Holy Spirit leads us into relationships with other believers. Again, there may come a time when we must separate from other believers, but it will be the last thing we do, not the first, and it will be after much patience and love have been demonstrated.

A good coach brings people together so the team can succeed. Allow for differing opinions when it's not an issue of salvation. Set the example for your people because others are watching. We need uncluttered Christianity. We need to get back to the real issues of faith.

I recognize that some of what you have read may upset you. I know that we as believers have differing opinions on so many things. My goal here is not to make everyone happy, because that is impossible. My goal is to say that for your team to succeed you need to be in agreement on what you believe. Make sure everyone knows what that is. Decide what matters to you and make sure everyone agrees. You have a conscience and you must follow it. If for you something is wrong, then it is wrong. You must also let some things go. Just make sure that you do not let go of the salvation issues or you will lose God's blessing.

PART 5

WE ARE THE CHAMPIONS!

16

RECRUITING NEW PLAYERS

Our Mission as God's Team

Good coaches know that the best defense is a good offense. In sports, a coach scouts the team they are going to play next, evaluates his or her own players, and then puts together a game plan to win based on these assessments.

In football, the team you are playing may have a great run defense, so you assess whether you can change your attack to meet the weakness of the opponent. Ultimately a coach would try to develop a well-balanced team that can take advantage of any weakness, but in reality every team has natural strengths and weaknesses that can be exploited.

This applies to God's team as well. Remember, the goal of God's team is to win. We win when we attack the culture with our thinking, energy, resources, and abilities. The goal: to take territory from the enemy. The objective: souls restored to their Creator. God's team, the church, is not just hiding out from the enemy. In coach's language, we are trying to build the program. We are trying to recruit new players for the team.

God's team has many players, each with skills to contribute. Unfortunately, many of God's coaches have an incorrect view of the teams they coach. I believe that God has supplied every team with what it needs to meet the enemy in the area they live in. It is so sad to see that God has amply supplied all that is needed to reach each uniquely different community, but His coaches are not recognizing the needs or the abilities given. Often, we are so busy trying to keep team members from killing one another that we don't give them an enemy to fight or a game to play.

I believe that the job of the coach is to rally the troops to attack the need in a given place. That need will be different in each diverse culture, or area, but there is a need. Jesus makes it clear that we are to look out for and care for the hurting. Scripture tells us that pure and undefiled religion is to care for the widows and orphans. Jesus said that to care for the least is to care for Him.

The early church understood this and was known for ministering to the people around them. The early church was not waiting for people to come to them; they were aggressively moving into the world. They were caring for the hurting, and it opened the door to the hearts of the lost.

REACHING YOUR COMMUNITIES

I have four recommendations for church leaders who want to reach their communities. These recommendations come from my own experience at Real Life.

First, pray that God will reveal to you how He would have you reach the area where you live. There are many ways to reach out, but God must show you how to use your players and their energies right now. Timing is a big part of how successful a ministry will be. Twice before, groups had come to the Coeur d'Alene area to plant a church like ours. Both times they failed. I believe God wanted to start a church here, but it had to be the right time with the right people. Just because you have a good idea doesn't mean it is God's idea or His timing.

Second, vision-cast as a leader the idea that God has given you a mission and every person is an important part of it. God chose uneducated fishermen as disciples, which demonstrates that we are all qualified to serve, as long as we are filled with the Spirit of God. Christians have gotten used to believing the pastor is the special one with all the ideas and abilities. Show them they can all serve God. Be dream releasers.

Third, as you do this, people will start to share those dreams with you and the leadership. New ideas for outreach will rise to the top. Your job is to figure out which are Spirit-led ideas. The question is, with your support and the resources of the church committed, could the team pull off that idea? Is it God's plan or just a good idea?

Fourth, you must take the ideas that are given and discern if the need is real or imagined. For example, it would be unwise to put a youth ministry outreach in a retirement community. It is silly to start a food pantry in an affluent area just because it worked in the inner city. Evaluate the needs of the community in which you live. If there is a high alcohol and drug rate and no one is seriously dealing with the issue, then that may be your open door. If you live in an urban area, or an area that is struggling with the loss of jobs, you may have an open door through a food or clothing room or a thrift store. If you live in a community that enjoys the great outdoors where sports seems to be the interest of most of the people, an outreach program through sports and outdoor activities may bring an opportunity to reach lost people. Your job is to think outside the box, to evaluate the enemy's turf and figure out how to invade it.

Remember, you can only do so much. Your church only has so much energy and resources, so you must be careful to choose your attack carefully. It is better to do a few things well than do a lot poorly.

No "I" in Team

Often God's coaches respond negatively to those who might have new ideas about how to reach a community. They are often so busy preparing for the show, managing all of the spiritual infants in a church, doing funerals and weddings, that they can barely manage what they already have going on. You can see the flaw in their thinking as they say, "I have no time for that." Remember, the job of a coach is to get other gifted people to play the positions they are gifted for. If the coach is busy playing all the positions, he won't have time for anything new.

As you start to reach out in your community, remember that the end goal is to bridge your people to the discipleship process. If all you do is move people from the world to the church service, you have fallen short of discipling those you attracted. These people need relationships that help them grow.

Everyone in the Right Position

As you put together your outreach ministry, remember that some of the people on your team will be gifted in that area. Some will be effective teachers and will have a passion for women's, men's, seniors, or youth ministries. Some will enjoy serving in the nursery while others will enjoy stacking chairs. There is somewhere for everyone to minister. Your job is to make sure that a process is developed that takes people from the world all the way to maturity through relationship and service. When we put it all together, everyone is being used and people are growing because they are learning to play a part on God's team.

17

THE GROWING COACH

Learning from Mistakes, Always Improving

Every organization, like every person, runs the risk of becoming stagnant. As Christians we recognize that we're in a never-ending process. Like the apostle Paul, we know we have yet to reach perfection, but we will continue to press on toward the goal. Great teams are always about improvement. Last year was last year. We have to do it again, and more.

Most of us don't like change, and we don't like to grow, unless it doesn't hurt. It's our nature to stay comfortable. We avoid self-improvement, and because of that, excellence isn't possible. We want the Lord to affirm us rather than change us.

As a coach, I'm happy when the team is doing well, but I know there are always ways to improve. Great organizations encourage their players to carry on the mission to which they have committed themselves, always striving for greatness. If we have the "we have arrived" attitude, it won't be long before we become complacent.

Worse yet, we may begin the downward spiral of self-destruction; pride comes before a fall.

EVALUATION AND SELF-ASSESSMENT

Every coach wants to build within the framework of the organization a culture of excellence. I want our people to ask, "What did we learn? How can we do better next time?" I don't want to be a perfectionist who can never be pleased with our effort or outcomes, but I do want to keep growing.

In order to build this value into the team, the coach must model it. He must evaluate his own performance and allow others to evaluate it as well. We coaches are often either too hard on ourselves or not hard enough. Either way, it's rare that any of us have a true perception of self. The only way to truly assess our own performance accurately is to seek and listen to the leading of the Holy Spirit and to others God has placed in our lives as teammates.

PEER EVALUATION

A growing leader needs input. A coach must allow others to evaluate him; there must be a culture of accurate assessment in an organization. A coach must become vulnerable and positive when he receives honest feedback, or the process ends right there. Unfortunately, leaders are often intimidating. Whether or not he or she means to be, the coach can be seen as the one you should never question, at least not face-to-face. The higher someone is up the ladder, the less feedback he usually receives. Often, the feedback a pastor does receive is skewed toward the positive. This can be dangerous because such a person could begin to believe his own press and become proud.

An accurate and honest assessment encourages better leadership. In order to improve, constructive criticism is essential. When we accept our faults correctly, as something that can be changed, rather than seeing ourselves as complete failures, we are able to grow.

A Test in Perception

Not long ago we developed a test for individuals to figure out where they were weak so they could improve. This test evaluates people in eighteen areas of leadership competency. We call it The Summit.

The Summit is not an evaluation you give yourself; rather, it is the result of feedback from those who know you best: your co-workers, those you lead, your friends, your family, and your spouse; some may even go to the elders of the church. This test relies solely upon honesty. The questions are designed to reveal areas of consistent strengths and weaknesses. The test includes questions like, "Would you follow this person into war? Why or why not?" It quickly draws the evaluator into the heart of leadership issues.

To be involved in this evaluation, you have to be one who strives for excellence, desires improvement, and is willing to be vulnerable to criticism. You have to be willing to be evaluated by the people who know you best.

I took The Summit and found out how people perceived me. Since I want to create an environment where others feel it's okay to make mistakes and be real, I was relieved and glad to know people see me as authentic.

Strengths have a flip side, an area of potential weakness. I learned I'm perceived as a person who lacks emotional self-control. In other words, if I'm emotionally down, people know it, and if I'm up, they know that too. If I don't like something, they can see it on my face. If I fail, everyone knows. They view me as reactionary, basing my action on my emotions. I scored high on influence, which can be an asset but, coupled with my lack of emotional self-control, could be a recipe for disaster. I could potentially bring the whole place down when I'm tired or having a bad day.

This realization was my wake-up call. I recognized that I'd placed a great deal of value on being real, but that could damage my team when not applied in the right way or balanced with emotional self-control. Acknowledging my weaknesses didn't devastate me. Instead, I was motivated to improve!

As coaches, we must want to improve in order to create the environment where the team also seeks to improve. In order for a team to grow and win, we need to know how we are perceived as teammates with the staff. We also need to know how the congregation perceives us, because they will not follow a leadership that hasn't earned the right to lead. Such scrutiny might hurt, but it's necessary.

Whether or not we take a test, ask others to point out our weaknesses, seek wise counsel, or become approachable, we must continually strive for improvement. When a team values personal growth over comfort, they don't take good-intentioned criticism as an attack. They don't see coaching as a threat but as positive instruction, a way to improve.

Assessing Your Team

We have also created an assessment for churches. Before we assess a church, we have the staff pass out an evaluation/survey to their people. We ask that they be divided among those who have been a part of the church for many years, those who have been attending for just a few years, and those who have just started attending, including visitors.

The evaluations are returned to us anonymously, weeks in advance of our training session so we can tally the numbers and provide an accurate summary of how the leadership is perceived. On this churchwide test, we evaluate things like coaching skills, "Do people feel led and inspired?"; shepherding ability, "Are the leaders loving, caring, and available?"; and authenticity, "Does the flock trust the leadership?"

When the leaders of the church arrive, we ask them to evaluate themselves, based on these same competencies. The findings are interesting; seldom do the congregation and lay leaders have the same perception as the staff. On the question that asks, "Would you follow these men into battle?" generally almost all agree that they would not. Most explain, "If I got hurt, I think they would just leave me on the field."

210

It's hard to see these men, who care, become disheartened. It's hard to watch them realize their sheep do not perceive them as caring shepherds. We ask them to formulate some conclusions and come up with a plan to change these perceptions.

One of the most interesting meetings we have had with a church revealed that the leadership was perceived as uncaring and the people were displeased. Of course, this took the staff by surprise. The staff had graded their friendliness and love for people high. When the senior pastor saw the results, his comment was, "Well, they [the congregation] are not very friendly either!"

We were blown away by his reaction. One of our staff members questioned him immediately. He asked, "Whose responsibility is it to set the tone in your church—who is the leader?" This pastor believed that he had been a good leader to his staff. He was unwilling to receive their evaluation; rather than change, he defended himself and lost his ministry a year later.

Becoming aware that there is a problem and accepting that something must be changed is a great deal of the battle, but we also must accept the need for accountability if we are going to improve. We all have deep ruts in our lives. Our past experiences and personalities make us susceptible to falling back into our old way of leading and living.

If we are to succeed, we must empower others around us to tell us when we fall back into old habits. It takes a lot of work to stay out of our old way of interacting with others. We need people who love us enough to keep us where our organization needs us to be.

RESENTMENT HINDERS IMPROVEMENT

As Christians, there is an added component we must deal with. We know we're supposed to forgive and extend grace, so rather than being honest with people we remain quiet. We tell ourselves, "I will let it go." We spiritualize our issues with people by saying,

"It's not right to criticize. I need to learn to be content no matter the circumstances."

While we shouldn't try to take the place of the Holy Spirit in another person's life by pointing out all their faults, we often rationalize away the real reason we choose not to confront: we are cowards. Because we don't deal with things as they come up, we become bitter. We say we will let it go, but we don't. We would rather harbor resentment than risk rejection.

The devil helps us assign motives to others that likely don't exist, and fear keeps us from learning the truth. We know we make mistakes unintentionally but tend to assume others acted intentionally. The result: not only does the leader not improve, but the enemy has a heyday with the one wronged. Bitterness builds and people may move on to another church instead of working things out. Or they stick around and spew their negativity. A few may stay and say nothing, but their spiritual growth will decline because they have allowed the enemy to steal their joy.

The Truth about Confrontation

We are told to confront others when we are offended (see Matt. 18:15). God's plan is to resolve issues as they come up. He desires reconciliation. How can there be reconciliation when the one offending has no idea he's done something? How can a new believer understand how a behavior may be normal for the world but has no place in the church, if people don't step up in love and resolve issues?

We see why the devil works against God's plan for resolution so aggressively. He doesn't want God's team to improve. He likes bitter roots to grow up in hearts and in churches. He hates unity; he loves factions and splits. He wants us to self-destruct in the locker room before we hit the field!

A coach must teach his or her people to do things biblically. Team conflict is a reality. How it's dealt with will determine success. Victory is achieved in the locker room and the huddle, not when you play the opponent. Make sure everyone has the right expectations and knows what to do when, not if, a problem occurs. Teach people to be honest with one another, speaking the truth in love (see Eph. 4:15), and to not leave until tomorrow what should be said today. Create a culture that values truth.

PROMOTING HONESTY AND RESOLUTION

If a culture of resolution is to be created, it starts with the leader. The leader must lead the way by dealing with issues immediately, lovingly, and truthfully. The leader must also allow others to confront him or her. It can be hard for people to confront a leader they respect; by being approachable and refusing to adopt an attitude of defensiveness, the leader can pave the way for those who would care enough to confront him. The leader must ask questions, look into people's eyes to see if there is something unsaid, and when confronted, the leader must accept it with respect.

Whether or not I agree with the person who voices the concern, in my mind they deserve respect for saying it to my face. When someone is this honest with me, I praise them for it. It is important to react in the right way, not defensively. When we deal with things in the right way, the news spreads quickly. People talk about it with other people, and we are well on our way to creating a culture that gives accurate assessments.

SPEAK THE TRUTH IN LOVE

As coaches, we must create an environment where people will *see* the truth *and speak it* in love. They need to recognize their own faults along with the faults of others in the context of a loving and encouraging family. People who are able to see their own weaknesses and failures are more likely to be gentle with others when they fail. When people are authentic, mutual accountability is formed through relationships. As a result, the shepherd cares for and sacrifices for his sheep. The flock of believers becomes a safe place for people to share their hearts, whether it is a word of encouragement or correction. We must not be a church that shoots its wounded. We must call sin what it is, but hate the sin and *not* the sinner.

Remember, the goal is to create a culture of honesty. Without honesty there will be little improvement and less blessing from the Lord. The coach must set the tone by being real. If the coach drifts from time to time, he or she has people who have been trained by example to be honest. It is hard to drift from the course when so many understand the goal and have been empowered to speak.

Playing Hard
without Getting
Hurt

Your Team and Change

If you've read this entire book, you've probably been challenged at some point. If you haven't, I've failed.

I don't expect you to agree with everything I've said, but if I've caused you to think, I have achieved one of my goals. For those of you who have agreed, you're probably faced with a dilemma. How do you implement change?

Some readers will have the luxury of starting fresh in a new church plant. Others will have to change existing organizations. How does that happen?

Change is never easy. In fact, for us it was incredibly hard! You may face added challenges—people who won't let you lead no matter what you do or people who won't follow because you have not been the leader you should have been.

Before changing an organization, some of us need to become coaches who can be followed. I learned this the hard way in my last ministry. Things might have been different if I had started changing first.

Change takes time, especially if you serve in an older church. A rapid change could cause a church split or worse, even if the newfound truth is what the church needs. It's important to get the rest of the leaders on board so they will understand why change is needed. And remember, big does not always mean progressive. The bigger the ship, the harder it is to turn. As leaders we must be very careful how we go about dealing with the Lord's church. I believe many churches need to change, but leaders must be wise about how they do it.

CHANGE STARTS WITH RELATIONSHIP

A pastor who wants to change an organization needs to understand that strategy is not what people follow. They follow a shepherd who has earned the right to be followed, who has demonstrated his love for his sheep and listened to the other shepherds on his team. He needs to include these leaders and allow them to be a part of the change.

Be there for your leaders when they are down. Celebrate their victories. A good leader earns respect as a result of his hard work and ability to serve. Jesus said, "He who would be first, must be last." He didn't mean don't lead. He meant you earn influence by serving, by being humble, by sharing praise, and by sharing responsibility. If you want to change your organization, you must first earn the trust of your people, especially of the other leaders in your church.

Before you attempt to change a church, you must have God's help. Prayer is essential to implementing change in the church. I have found that when our leadership prays, God works on hard hearts and He gives wisdom (see James 1:5). I recommend you pray with your leaders and for them.

Repair relationships within the leadership before you embark on a new destination. Don't make a move until you know you are going to be blessed by the Lord's presence because of your oneness of heart. Seek forgiveness from anyone you have wronged.

CASTING A VISION AND CREATING A PLAN

A godly vision is inspiring, especially one that can be backed up by Scripture. The good vision caster is filled with passion and embodies what he or she wants others to do. To implement change you must eat, sleep, and drink the vision. Develop a team in your congregation to fuel the vision of your church. Before your church will follow your lead, however, they have to know you love them.

Be sure to include your whole leadership team when it comes to the creation of a new plan. It is essential that they know why you need to change. They and their ideas should be included in the building of the plan, or they will not buy into it. Brainstorming is so important to building a complete, well-thought-out plan. All the leaders must be ready to act.

Don't forget to count the cost of the plan to your congregation. Be ready for those who will disagree. Take your ideas to the next level of leadership and then to the congregation. Allow your people time to ask questions and give input. Remember to spend time earning the right to lead by the way you act. If you haven't, this may take awhile, but it's worth it.

A WARNING

Whatever you do, remember, the church is not your church; it belongs to God. You don't have the right to split His church. If you've done all you can to change the church, but there's a significant number of leaders opposed to the direction you feel led to take, be careful. God's reputation is at stake, and when Christians fight, it causes unbelievers to reject Jesus. No matter what, always honor the church's leadership. Never allow those who work with you (who agree with you) to gossip about those who don't.

Of course, change can't be implemented when a leadership is divided in purpose and direction. But you have a choice to make. You can decide to focus on what is not happening, or you can be joyful that you are creating disciples in the areas where you work. You may have to leave because your principles do not allow you to be involved in a church that is not strategically doing what they should be. Just remember, those who oppose you might be wrong in their direction (or lack thereof), but it does not mean they are not fellow believers. If you decide to leave the church, leave in love and honor knowing that God will not bless you if you hurt His body and reputation.

CHANGE MAY MEAN YOU HAVE TO FIGHT

In a situation where your leadership has agreed to a change but there are some in the church who oppose it, you might have to fight. You might have to confront in love those who are divisive. In Matthew 18:15–20, God gives us rules for resolving conflict in the church. When a person of influence will not submit to leadership, it's likely that once you deal with the problem they will share their opinion with anyone who will listen.

You can't stand by and wait for the damage to occur. You'll need to do some damage control. If you've built a relationship with your people, you may be able to use your relational clout to stem the tide. But either way, you have to stop the cancer from spreading as quickly as you can. If the person is in leadership and refuses to submit to the rest of the leaders, you must take action. No fear! Pray and confront the person as a team. A good leader confronts issues as they occur.

Some allow those with money to control what happens because of fear of lost income. Remember, it's God's church and He owns the cattle on a thousand hills. Do what is right and He will provide.

ONLY THE FEW, ONLY THE COMMITTED

Sticking to the Mission No Matter What

As I draw to the end of this book, I want to leave you with a challenge. To be a leader on God's team is extremely challenging. I often asked myself, "What have I gotten myself into?" Let's remember we get to be a part of the most significant thing in history. We get to be a part of fighting for the eternal souls of men. We get to be on a team with the Eternal God. This cosmic war we are engaged in has been going on since the garden, and we already know who wins. Let's not forget who we are in Christ. Let's not forget the responsibility and privilege we have been given. Let's give it our all. I want to be able to say like Paul, I have fought the fight, I have finished the race, and now I have a crown waiting for me. Let's give our all on the field and teach those who follow us to do the same.

Nothing great happens unless great effort is exerted. Greatness will not be achieved unless you are willing to do what most are not. That is why greatness is a rare thing. I will never forget how I learned this lesson.

LESSONS FROM A GREAT COACH

It was my first day on the campus of North Idaho Junior College. I had received several scholarship offers to wrestle at bigger colleges, but I wanted to wrestle for John Owen. He had won more national championships and coached more All-Americans than I could count. He had more coach-of-the-year awards than he could fit on any one wall in his office. His reputation spoke volumes.

North Idaho was known all over the country as a wrestling powerhouse that supplied four-year schools with great talent. In fact, they wrestled and beat most of the four-year schools on the western side of the United States, so I would get my chance to shine. Having been a three-time state champion, I was used to winning and expected that to continue in college.

Coach Owen had asked all the wrestlers to show up a few days early so that we could have a team meeting before school got started. It was a balmy August day when I arrived in beautiful Coeur d'Alene, Idaho. As I met the guys I would room with, I must admit it felt as if I was coming home, rather than just leaving it. I had always felt a little bit different in high school. I had been like other kids in that I partied, but different in that I knew what I wanted out of life from my freshman year on. I was committed to training. I was focused on my goal to be the best in my sport. I was also somewhat crazy in the eyes of the people who knew me. I was tough, unafraid, and willing to do just about anything.

After meeting the guys and moving in to the wrestlers' scholarship house, it was time to head for the meeting in the gym. I knew right away I had come into a new world. I had always been the biggest and strongest in the little high school I had gone to, but as I walked into that room, I knew things had changed. These guys were the toughest-looking people I had ever seen. I thought *I* could cuss, but these people were on a different level. It took them thirty seconds longer to complete a simple sentence because of the expletives they added.

I really didn't know anyone, so I made my way to the corner of the room and sat where I could watch all those who entered. Most of the guys wore clothing that showed off their arms; they were intimidating, to say the least. Everyone was comparing notes, asking where others were from, finding out how many state titles each had won. Just like me, they were trying to figure out who they were going to have to beat to make the team. To be honest, one look at these guys told me that beating any of them would not be easy.

Ten minutes before the meeting started, the room was filled with about forty-five tough-looking, vile-talking maniacs. We were all in chairs gathered around long tables. As I was contemplating the new challenges before me, something strange happened. Six guys entered the room together. They were dressed nicer, not showing off their biceps, though you could tell they had them. They were quiet, displaying no interest in getting attention. They went to the back of the room, each carrying a duffle bag, where they quietly sat together.

The door opened again, and John Owen and his staff came into the room. The place became completely silent. Coach carried with him a trophy with names on it and a picture. Large bold letters formed the words "1985 Wrestling National Champions." The photo was of beaten and bruised warriors, grinning from ear to ear. They were all holding up one finger, standing as one, like a band of brothers locked arm in arm. They were the Champions.

Coach very quietly said, "For those of you who don't know me, I am Coach Owen and these are my assistants. You know that last year we won the team national championship. We had eight All-Americans out of the ten possible weight classes." He then went on to tell us what it was like to win a national team title. He told us about the team riding on the fire truck down the middle of Main Street, about the crowds, the glory, and all the scholarships to bigger colleges that the departing sophomores had received. He told us about how they had done something that would go down in history. He said that very few get to look back on their lives and remember that they had been the best at something. We were going to get an opportunity to have that kind of memory.

He surveyed those of us gathered in the room. "There are six returning All-Americans, about twenty state champions, and about fifteen who have won multiple state championships. The rest are walk-ons who have probably at least placed in state. The firepower in this room is powerful enough for us to win it all again. But in order for us to do it, we will have to become a team. Team is everything! Team is family. Though wrestling seems like an individual sport, no wrestler wins without good partners who push the starters to greatness. Wrestling is really a team sport. To win as a team we will need to decide who are the best at every weight class; then all ten starters will need to strive to become individual All-Americans. This means they will have to place in the top eight in their weights. They will have to do this while wrestling the best in the whole nation. Everyone on this team, starter or not, will have a part of that national trophy."

As Coach spoke, you could feel the temperature in the room start to rise. We were getting fired up.

REALISTIC DETERMINATION

Suddenly, something caught my eye that caused Coach's inspiring speech to fade for a moment. One of the six guys who had come in quietly just before the coach arrived leaned over in his chair with his head resting on the table in front of him. As Coach got further in his speech, this guy started to quietly, yet audibly, hit his head on the table. *Thump, thump, thump.* The others with him looked anything but fired up.

Coach Owen really started to get going, and it drew my attention away from the oddity sitting near me. "There are about fifty of you who have come out for the team this year, but only a small number sitting here will finish the season. There are only a few who have what it takes to be an All-American this year. Some will stick it out and be an All-American next year, but most of you will quit."

His voice became quiet but intense, filled with emotion. "I have a question for you. Who in this room wants to be an All-American?" Some of the guys responded audibly, all of us nodded. *Of course I do*, I thought, *or I wouldn't be here.*

He said, "Maybe you did not understand my question. How many want to be an All-American? Let me hear you!" We all responded this time. Coach looked at one of the assistant coaches standing next to him and said, "Maybe we have the wrong guys in this room." He then looked at us again and said, "Maybe you don't get it. How many want to be an All-American!"

This time we were on our feet, shouting "I do!" at the top of our lungs. Again, something strange caught my eye. Over at the table with the six guys, no one was standing. They were all sitting quietly except the one guy, who was still hitting his head on the table.

Coach said, "It sounds like you are ready to get started then. Here is what I want you to do. You have one hour to go home and get your running shoes and be back here. We are going to load up in vans and we are going to take you to a hill where you will run three miles. If you do not make it in twenty-one minutes, we will put you back in the van and take you to the beginning so you can run it again until you make it or quit. We will do this every day for two weeks, then we will move it up to five miles, for time. We will do that for about a month until we will have a thirteen-mile run, for time. For everyone who makes it, your gear will be waiting at the end."

Coach went on to say, "After running today and every other day, you will come back here and we will wrestle. You will also lift every morning, and we will check your attendance at the weight room door. This will go on until the season officially starts, and then we will have a really tough regimen for you to follow. You will run, lift, and wrestle every day. You will also watch films and have to make weights that you will wrestle your teammates for. You will also be required to pass twelve credits in school with at least a 2.0 grade point average, so that will require some real study. In other words, gentlemen, your life has just changed!"

223

Coach then said something that has stayed with me over the years: "Most people will never be great at anything. They have no desire to do more than just get by. They will never even try to do something great, because they don't care about anything enough to put it all out there. Others like the idea of being great, in your case becoming an All-American. They like the thought of the glory, they like the idea of wearing a national champion letterman's jacket, and they also like the thought of being interviewed for the paper or on television. Many of you like the dream, but I know that not many of you will do what it takes to be great. It will take too much sacrifice. You won't be able to do what all the other college students can do. You won't be able to party all the time. You won't be able to go to Taco Bell at midnight with your friends, because you will have weight to lose. You will be exhausted from wrestling, and then you will have to study. We have fifty guys here, but we'll probably end up with thirty, and those thirty will be able to make history."

He continued. "Before we let you go, we want to introduce our six returning All-Americans. Guys, come forward." Much to my amazement, the six quiet guys who had come in together came forward, including the one who had been thumping his head on the table.

It was at this point that I realized why John, as I came to know him later, had been hitting his head on the table. I realized why they had their duffle bags with them. They had heard this all before. They, unlike all of us new guys, knew what was coming next. John knew the dream to be an All-American came with a price—a price he had already paid once and was ready to pay again. He knew it would be painful, and his head-thumping revealed that he was not really looking forward to it.

As I look back on that day, I learned a very important lesson. Greatness costs, sometimes more than we want it to. Coach was wrong. We ended up with only twenty-three when it was all over, but all twenty-three won the national team title. We all worked together, starters and workout partners, working together for a common cause. Our starters won the national title by doubling the point total of the nearest team.

A GREATER CHAMPIONSHIP

I remember those times fondly, because I learned so many lessons that have stayed with me. I remember feeling like there was nothing more important than becoming an All-American. I wanted so badly to be the best and to be on a team that won it all.

Now I look back, and I know that I learned what it means to put everything you have into something and to see others do the same. But now I also feel kind of silly. I was willing to work that hard for a crown that would not last. I was willing to commit myself to something that very few would care about later.

Not many years ago, when I coached in Oregon, we were at the state championships, and my high school team was sitting together far up in the bleachers of the arena. It was the championship finals, and all the usual pomp and circumstance was going on below. The boys were messing around, not paying attention to what was happening below as they honored the Hall of Fame wrestlers in the state of Oregon. All of these men had won state titles, and most had won national college titles in their day. Most of the crowd was not watching. Oh, some were politely applauding, but most were ready to get to their matches. My team had many who had placed in state, and some who were wrestling for state titles that night. Almost all of them were committed to the sport and had worked hard not only all year but for many years just to be in the tournament.

As the ceremony below was being ignored, I gathered the guys and asked them why they were not paying attention to the old guys who were being honored below. They said things like, "We don't know them" and "We don't care." I asked them why they were working so hard for something that future young wrestlers, just like them, would not care about either. It was quiet, but they got my point. I then asked them what they were going to do with their lives that future generations would respect, unlike what was going on below.

As I remember my North Idaho days, I think about so many lessons learned. Coach Owen was right when he said that most don't care enough about anything to give everything. We all like the idea of winning but aren't willing to commit to the lifestyle.

225

GOD'S TEAM

As I look at my job as coach of God's team, it's easy to forget that I am involved in something so much more important than winning a national wrestling championship. God's coaches get to be involved in His mission to save the world. He allows us to join Him as He seeks to fight a battle for the souls of men. In the halls of heaven's courts, the battles we win now will be remembered forever. The trophies are not made of metal or plastic. The adoring crowd that cheered for me as I wrestled but later forgot so easily are not like the ones that cheer us on in this spiritual battle. The ones who watch us from the heavenly stands make up the great cloud of witnesses who are with the Father, remembering forever.

Sometimes, as I look at God's people, I wonder if they really care about anything. They don't seem to be too excited about winning anything except their personal comfort and glory. The lost go on uninvited and unimpressed by our commitment level. They don't seem to want to join a team where the players are not passionate about winning.

People who are sold out to a cause are inspiring because they are willing to put up with anything to achieve the dream. We admire their passion, their stamina, their courage, especially when they are fighting for a noble cause. As I watch God's players, I often wonder, "What is their mission? Do they have one at all?" They show up for the team meeting and cheer with the crowd, yet they have no intention of finishing what they started. They like hanging around the team, being associated with the players, but will never do what it takes to win.

REASONS FOR QUITTING

As I watched my talented teammates quit that year, I mentally collected the most common reasons. Over the years, I have watched many leave God's team for the same reasons.

First, people leave because they were never really committed to the team and the mission in the first place. It was a good idea, but it was a conditional commitment. They were not committed to the coach as the authority, rule maker, and expert, and they had not decided that a wrestler was really what they were. In the spiritual realm, many have not really accepted the spiritual reality that Jesus is Lord, that the Word is the rulebook, and that there is a war going on. They go to church but are not part of the church. They believe in Christ but are not Christians. They like the idea but are not committed to the lifestyle.

Second, people leave because of an unwillingness to sacrifice personal desires to attain the goal. A good example for a wrestler would be food. Some wrestlers are not willing to give up what they want to eat for what they should eat so that they and the team can win. Nothing great happens, in sports or in the church, without great discipline.

Third, people leave because they are unwilling to do what they don't want to do. There are times when you must push yourself beyond your comfort zone. You must run when you don't want to. You must lift when you don't want to. You must keep going though every part of you says stop. How many Christians are willing to expend a similar amount of effort for God?

Fourth, people leave because the going gets tough. I watched wrestlers who had won championships in high school quit because they could not immediately win in college. They did not see losing as a lesson that if learned well could propel them to greatness. Christians too can learn from their failures, but often they walk off God's team, despondent and forever defeated.

STICKING TO THE MISSION

And then there's a guy like Kevin, the only other Idaho kid on my team back then. Kevin walked on with no scholarship. His first challenge match to make the first team ended in embarrassment. He lost by technical fall (a fifteen-point margin) in the first round. But the next week he challenged the same guy again. He made it a little longer into the first round. Halfway through the season he made it through the whole match, and he was ecstatic. By the end of the season he had beaten the kid and had taken his place. That year he became an All-American, taking fourth in the nation. He went on to place four times. I have never seen a harder worker.

God honors commitment. God doesn't always use the most talented, but He does use the most committed. So often I watch young pastors come out of the chute, hot to change the world. Then they get a reality check. Like me, they realize the church is in trouble and they try to fix it, only to get hammered. So they quit. They forget that God called them to coach. They give up without trying to figure out what went wrong so they can change it.

In this battle we are in, we don't have the option of quitting. How can we quit, knowing what Jesus has done? How can we quit when we have peered into the spiritual world and know people are at risk of going to hell?

Some players stay on the team, but they never really win because they are not willing to learn. Several of the North Idaho wrestlers worked with Coach Owen as assistants at an area-wide wrestling camp during the summers. I will never forget the time Coach Owen walked up to a junior high wrestler who was incorrectly doing the move just demonstrated. He kindly tried to correct the kid, but the boy would have none of it. I could not believe what I was hearing. This kid told Coach Owen that he did not do it that way. He had a way of doing things that worked for him. He wasn't going to change, even though he was absolutely wrong.

That kid had the opportunity to be coached by a person who had shaped national champions, but he would not listen because he thought he knew better. The kid's explanation was that it had worked on all the little kids he had wrestled. Coach tried to explain to him that it would not work on an experienced, older wrestler. The kid refused to listen, so Coach just moved away to work with someone who would listen.

Many hold on to what they like rather than what works. I am not talking about breaking the rules to win. I am saying that there are better ways to get some things done. Maybe we learned something from a past mentor that we have committed ourselves to, though it doesn't really work. Maybe we figured some things out on our own that enable us to win for a while or in some specific, minor situations. These things may have worked then, but they may not carry us through to the tougher and bigger engagements on the battlefield.

I believe God gives us those who can help us if we are willing to learn and listen. God wants His team to take new ground, which means we will have to learn and grow. I believe that God wants us to win, that He wants to build an unbeatable team. He is looking for players who will be committed. He is looking for coaches who will stick around no matter what. In 2 Chronicles 16:9, Scripture tells us, "For the eyes of the LORD range throughout the earth to strengthen those whose hearts are fully committed to him." He doesn't need excessive talent. He likes to use little people to do big things. He gets all the glory when He uses people the world wouldn't look twice at.

People will model your kind of commitment. They will see your passion and either be drawn to what you are drawn to, or they will believe you aren't all in, so why should they be. You are called to a personal battle that will take all you have to win.

PLAY HARD

During my years as an athlete and coach, I never wanted to win an athletic championship as badly as I want to win on this team. This game to be played and won is for eternity.

God has given us all a great team, a good game plan, and the strength to win. All the pieces are there. All we as coaches have to do is go out and use them, teaching our people to work as a team.

As a coach I have much to learn as I continue to walk with the Lord. I know if I'm faithful, giving Him all the glory for the successes He gives, we can finish this race and be a part of His eternal plan.

I recognize that God is never done with any of us. Since this book was started and nearly completed, the Lord has been giving our team new insights and further direction. As usual, God brings people into our lives that help us to take the next steps. God connected us with Avery Willis, a man who understands discipleship. Avery is the author and developer of *MasterLife: A Biblical Process for Growing Disciples*. He served for ten years as a pastor in Oklahoma and Texas and as a missionary for fourteen years in Indonesia. He was the senior vice-president of overseas operations at the International Mission Board of the Southern Baptist Convention. He later served as the director of the Adult Department of the Discipleship and Family Development Divisions, the Sunday School Board of the SBC (now LifeWay Christian Resources), where he introduced the Lay Institute for Equipping (LIFE), a series of in-depth discipleship courses. He has authored a number of books, including *MasterBuilder: Multiplying Leaders*, and coauthored the book *On Mission with God* with Henry Blackaby. He has pointed us to a new and more effective way of teaching in our small groups using storying.

The church world recognizes that biblical literacy is at new lows. We recognize that few have a biblical worldview, and few know what to do about it. The old way of teaching the Bible is less effective as our culture becomes more visual—more story driven. In the last year Real Life has embarked on a new strategy to use what is working in disciple-making movements around the world. We are using Orality as the basis for teaching in our small groups. Orality is a method of using stories as the main vehicle for teaching the Bible in the discipleship process. Every culture in the world uses stories as a way to transmit family history, values, etc. Storytelling is an art form. Hollywood has mastered it in our culture.

As a church, we are seeking to develop a way to create leaders who can accurately teach theology and biblical history to our disciples. Few of our small group leaders are gifted teachers, but all, whether parents or leaders, are called to make disciples. The storytelling method resonates with this culture, especially since most no longer learn exclusively through literary methods. All of our people can tell a Bible story and ask good questions. It leads to better participation and better learning. Those at Real Life who have always felt unqualified to lead now say, "I can do this." We have found that our people are not only learning the Bible, but they are making better disciples. The groups are becoming fun. Believe it or not, our disciples are getting their theology right as well. I encourage you to look into this strategy, as we are.

❖

I hope this journey has challenged you to seek truth. I hope as you have read this book that you have understood my heart. We, as the church worldwide, need to be on a mission—a mission to save the world. It's a battle we must win. It's a matter of life and death.

God bless you as you go on your journey. Pray for us as we go on ours. May God's team kick the enemy's fanny. In Jesus' name. Amen.

Appendix

Practice, Play, Win!

A Guide for Individual or Group Reflection and Implementation

These questions are designed to help readers digest and apply these ideas to their local settings either individually or in a small group.

Introduction—The Real Life Story

Practice...

- List three ways God moved people or circumstances to begin the work in Post Falls, Idaho.
- Describe how the value of shepherding affected the way ministry developed at Real Life.

Play...

- If leaders from outside were to observe your church on an average week, what do you think they would conclude about the philosophy that drives your church's ministry?
- Is the philosophy that drives your ministry simple enough that it can be reproduced by others?

Win!

- Reflect on the opening chapters of Acts. How was God active in this setting?
- After reading this chapter and responding to the above questions, what are the directions that you think your ministry would benefit from that have gone unnoticed up to this point?
- What roadblocks are hindering these things from happening?

CHAPTER 01—SWITCHING JERSEYS: A PASTOR'S JOURNEY

Practice...

- Working with kids in ministry brought a feeling of being "really alive." What aspects of your early experience in ministry made you feel that way?
- What was it about teaching school that highlighted the value of eternal things in this chapter?

Play...

- What things have you seen being done by churches that a good high school or college coach would never allow on the sports field?

- How is Jim's journey to church leadership similar to yours? How is it different?

Win!

- The analogy of coaching a sports team is helpful for finding solutions to ministry problems. Can you think of some problems in your church's ministry that the coaching analogy could help you address?
- Make a short list of good coaching practices. How are each of these practices supported or ignored in your church?

CHAPTER 02—CHASING A DREAM: LOOKING FOR THE WINNING CHURCH

Practice...

- If the church in America were an NFL team, what challenges would a new coach face?
- What keeps a good coach from giving up and quitting?

Play...

- What battles do you think the enemy has your church fighting that have little or nothing to do with winning?
- We often fight the right fights the wrong way. How have you avoided this mistake? How have you fallen into it?

Win!

- How do you define *winning* in your church?
- How does your definition of winning compare to the kind of victory suggested in this chapter?
- If you were to be part of the solution, what kind of behaviors and attitudes would be necessary?

CHAPTER 03—AND THE SCOREBOARD SAYS . . . : HOW ARE WE DOING?

Practice . . .

- According to this chapter, what are some of the signs of Christian maturity?
- What role does a building play in being a winning church?

Play . . .

- What was troubling about the flower analogy used to explain the state of the church in America? Do you agree with the speaker's conclusions?
- What do statistics reveal about the state of the church in America?

Win!

- This chapter highlights the disconnect of Christians from effective discipleship. How were you discipled?
- How did the way you were discipled prepare you to be different from the world in which you live?
- How does the way you disciple others prepare them to be part of a winning team?

CHAPTER 04—MISSION POSSIBLE: GOD'S TEAM CAN AND SHOULD WIN

Practice . . .

- What are the two conclusions Jim deduces from Jesus's statement to Peter in this chapter?

Play...

- What conclusions would people draw regarding the state of the church from listening to your conversations about the church?
- How does remaining in Christ affect the direction of your church and its efforts?

Win!

- Prayerfully consider your trust in Christ's statement: "The gates of hell will not prevail against it."
- Has your church defined winning in a way that Christ would not? How are the two definitions similar or different from one another?

CHAPTER 05—WINNING STARTS AT THE TOP: THE NEED FOR COACHES IN THE CHURCH

Practice...

- What is meant by the term "paid player"? Why is the whole idea of "paid players" a problem in the church?
- What are pastors often taught about the "Big Four" criteria for a successful church?

Play...

- To what degree is "The Show" a priority in your ministry? Could people in your church get the idea that their job is to attend the show?
- What is the difference between attending the church and being the church?

Win!

- Review your weekly schedule. What percentage of your time is spent on preparation and planning for what happens on Sunday morning? What percentage is spent on building players in relationships that transform them?
- Review your church budget. What percentage of your resources is designated to staff and equipment that primarily focus on the show? What percentage is spent on building players in relationships that transform them?

CHAPTER 06—A COACH WORTH FOLLOWING: DISCOVERING OUR GOD-GIVEN PURPOSE

Practice...

- What do great coaches possess that many knowledgeable leaders do not?
- What reality is important for a new Christian to be taught?
- What is the point of the story about the sheep talking to each other?

Play...

- If new believers are going to grow into devoted disciples, what role must the leaders play in their lives?
- As you read through Ezekiel 34, how do the prophet's words speak into the church in America?

Win!

- Prayerfully consider your heart as a shepherd. What issues hinder you from shepherding your people? What limitations hinder you from raising up leaders who shepherd your people?

Chapter 07—Good Recruiting: Outreach Events, Programs, and Weekend Services

Practice...

- What are some good examples of bridge events?
- What should the purpose of a worship service be?

Play...

- What aspect of your Sunday morning program is the strongest? The weakest?

Win!

- What is the greatest heartfelt concern of the staff and volunteers who you serve with on a Sunday morning?
- How much of a priority to your leadership is building relationships, and how is it expressed on Sunday morning? List the behaviors that support your conclusion.
- Would most of your people's neighbors feel comfortable coming to your services?

Chapter 08—Filling Out the Roster: Players Are Made, Not Born

Practice...

- What is the job of coaches on God's team?
- What difference was highlighted between high school and college coaches, and how does it apply to building a staff at church?

Play . . .

- Why do you think many pastors are reluctant to put their trainees into action before they have taught them everything that they believe is important?
- Does looking for players outside of your church work well most of the time? How much training would a future leader need to build disciples if you were always in relationship with him or her along the way?

Win!

- What have the leadership training efforts at your church produced in the last five years?
- Are there leaders right under your nose whom you have been passing over, assuming they would never become staff? If so, make a list of who they might be.

CHAPTER 09—IN THE HUDDLE: THE ESSENTIAL ROLE OF SMALL GROUPS

Practice . . .

- What limitations to learning are common in a large lecture setting?
- List some of the ways Jesus modeled effective discipleship.

Play . . .

- What are the four aspects of small groups that help make disciples?
- How can small groups remedy the limitations of a traditional lecture/sermon model?
- What is essential for a disciple-making small group?

Win!

- If your church currently has small groups, list the ways you think disciples are being made through them.
- If your church does not have small groups, or if your small groups are more of a program than the DNA of your church, how might they be transformed into better places for disciple making? List the top three things that you think would have the greatest impact in terms of small groups.

CHAPTER 10—THE CHAMPIONSHIP PROGRAM: A REPRODUCIBLE STRATEGY FOR LEADERSHIP DEVELOPMENT

Practice...

- Review the definition of a disciple. How do these qualities strike you? What do your responses reveal about your definition of discipleship?
- Summarize in your own words the differences between Share, Connect, Minister, and Disciple levels.

Play...

- What is the definition of *disciple* in your church?
- What process is followed to move people to the next level of maturity and growth?
- How is your process similar to the one given in this chapter? What is different about your process?

Win!

- Ask seven to ten leaders what their definition of a disciple is and how they understand the process of moving people through a process of discipleship.

- Take the responses and compare them to each other and to what the author is saying. What do you see? What needs to be done?

CHAPTER 11—PUTTING THE ROOKIE IN: TURNING PLAYERS LOOSE

Practice . . .

- What responsibilities go beyond the group meeting for small group leaders?

Play . . .

- How does being "in the game" affect those who are accustomed to sitting in pews?
- How does being "in the game" help people become personally vested?
- How does sitting on the bench hinder a person's commitment to the team's winning?

Win!

- Who in your church could be in the game at some level, but is not?
- What or who hinders them from moving off of the bench and on to the field?
- Make a list of those people's names. Pray for them this week with the game in mind. See what God does to you and to them.

CHAPTER 12—READING FROM THE SAME PLAYBOOK: HOW TO ALIGN YOUR TEAM FOR VICTORY

Practice...

- How does the illustration of differing playbooks shed light on the struggles that many churches have?
- How have pastors been set up for confusion by going to a conference that has all of the answers for their church?

Play...

- What process does your church use to get people using the same playbook?
- How is vision casting done for your people?
- What means are used to maintain focus for your leaders?

Win!

- After reviewing your process for getting people on the same playbook and keeping them focused, what is that process currently producing?
- Is your process constructed to accommodate a continuous flow of people through it?

CHAPTER 13—CHURCH IS A TEAM SPORT: CREATING A CULTURE OF TEAMWORK

Practice...

- What was the warning about pride, and how was it applied to teamwork?
- What are the four benefits of joint leadership given in this chapter? Do you see more?

Play...

- What do you believe is the biggest hindrance to shared leadership?
- What does teamwork look like in your church?
- How does a sermon club help in sermon preparation?
- How do you feel about the idea of a shared pulpit?

Win!

- Creating a culture of teamwork often involves deep heart issues that require time and prayerful consideration. What limits you or your staff from experiencing team at a deep level?

CHAPTER 14—WHEN THE GOING GETS TOUGH: GETTING REAL WITH EACH OTHER

Practice...

- How does unity provide a venue for leaders to be real and to be in relationship with each other?
- Why do ministers have few, if any, genuine relationships?
- What risks do pastors run by becoming isolated relationally?

Play...

- How do your staff and elders model authentic relationship to the volunteer leaders? How is it modeled to members?
- What must a good coach do to create and sustain an environment where authentic relationships thrive?

Win!

- Look at the relationships you have in your leadership. Rate the depth of those relationships on a one-to-five scale, with one being shallow and five being authentic.
- What problems do you encounter in leadership that can be traced to the source of unhealthy relationships? What could be done to improve those relationships?

CHAPTER 15—FOCUSING ON THE FUNDAMENTALS: THE IMPORTANCE OF UNCLUTTERED CHRISTIANITY

Practice...

- What is meant by the phrase "Fight like the devil for the things of God?" In what ways have you experienced this in your ministry?
- What is meant by the term "uncluttered Christianity"?

Play...

- How has division hurt new believers and unsaved people the most?
- In your mind, what is the difference between an essential doctrine and a non-salvation issue?

Win!

- What teachings of your church are worth dividing over? Which ones are not?
- How can you make sure the members of your church know the difference between essentials and non-salvation issues?

Chapter 16—Recruiting New Players: Our Mission as God's Team

Practice...

- What are the four factors to consider when we make a plan to reach our community?
- What hinders leaders/coaches in the church from considering new ideas for outreach and developing the people needed to implement them?

Play...

- What should each outreach bridge people to become?
- What is the role of the coach in this kind of approach to outreach?

Win!

- What are the dominant interests or characteristics of your community? How might those characteristics and interests be met or cooperated with to bridge people from your community to a disciple-making process?
- Take an inventory of your last month's schedule. How much of your time has been given to managing the Sunday morning "show," and how much has been given to developing ideas and people toward reaching the community?

Chapter 17—The Growing Coach: Learning from Mistakes, Always Improving

Practice...

- What hinders people from gaining an accurate self-assessment?
- What is the purpose of The Summit?

- How is accurate feedback affected as a person moves up the ladder of leadership?

Play...

- How did a lack of emotional self-control and a high aptitude toward influence create a potential problem?
- What resentment or bitterness have you experienced due to an avoidance of confrontation?
- Generally, how do you respond when confronted?

Win!

- This chapter places a great deal of emphasis on the ability and willingness of a team to gain an accurate picture of how they are perceived by others. What vehicles does your team use to maintain accurate feedback on their performance and reputation as leaders?
- If you were to find that people were not willing to follow you into battle, what do you think your initial response would be? How would your team process such a discovery?

CHAPTER 18—PLAYING HARD WITHOUT GETTING HURT: YOUR TEAM AND CHANGE

Practice...

- Where should change start?
- Why would it be important to include the leadership team in making a plan for change?
- Why is it important to remember who the church belongs to?

Play...

- Review the book, noting any marks or folded pages you may have left in previous chapters. Make a list of all the ideas from this book or that came to you as you read that you believe would help your team be better at winning.

Win!

- Share your list with a trusted leader. Find someone who will sit with you and allow you to explain your entire list. Bring clarity to the list based on your dialogue.
- Give your top three ideas to your leadership team. With their input, develop a plan that includes a lot of prayer, then take the first step.

CHAPTER 19—ONLY THE FEW, ONLY THE COMMITTED: STICKING TO THE MISSION NO MATTER WHAT

Practice...

- What inspires you to greatness for God's team? How often is that inspiration kindled and rekindled?
- Do you think it's true that most people don't care enough about anything to give everything?

Play...

- Review the reasons that were given for quitting. How have you experienced them? What others might you add to the list?
- How have you been kept from giving up? What encourages you and others to continue?

Win!

- How much does your leadership team care about winning God's battle in this world? What are you doing to give everything toward God's mission? What efforts are winning? What efforts are not?
- What "moves" are you possibly holding on to that are not working? What game plan would help you get coached to better moves?

Jim Putman served as a youth minister for nine years in two small churches (under 180 people) where he saw the youth ministries grow from under five to over a hundred. He also served as a wrestling coach in the public high school system where he received coach-of-the-year honors and led his teams to district titles and also coached several kids to state championships.

Jim Putman wrestled at North Idaho College and Western Montana College and graduated from Boise State University. Jim was a three-time college All-American in wrestling, reaching the national championship match twice. He was also a part of two national championship teams in college. He graduated from college with a bachelor degree in Social Science/Education, and later went to Boise Bible College and graduated with a bachelor in Bible.

Jim Putman is now the senior pastor of Real Life Ministries in Post Falls, Idaho. Real Life Ministries was started in October 1998 with a few families. Since that time, the church has grown to 8,000 in weekly attendance. There have been 1,800 baptisms in the last three years, and Real Life Ministries has over 600 small groups with more than 6,500 attending these groups weekly. Real Life has become the fastest-growing church in the Pacific Northwest (even though only 100,000 people live within a thirty-minute drive). Real Life has also started four new churches during the last three years, each being led by a person trained from within the congregation. One of the churches in nearby Spokane, Washington, is three years old and running 1,000, with a majority of their people in small groups as well.

Jim's greatest joy is to spend time with his family. He and his wife, Lori, have been married for eighteen years and are the parents of three boys—Christian, Jesse, and Will.

Correspondence may be sent to:
Jim Putman
c/o Real Life Ministries
1866 N. Cecil Rd.
Post Falls, Idaho 83854
http://www.reallifeministries.com

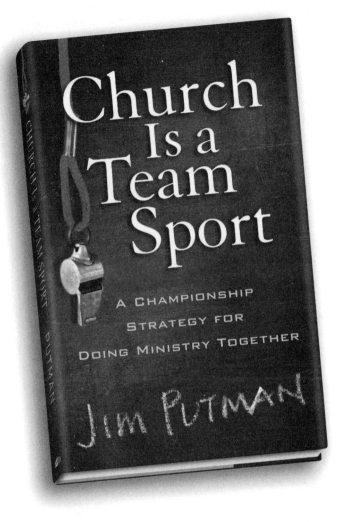

Visit

www.**churchisateamsport**.com

for videos and other tools to help you and your church
implement the strategies of Jim Putman's book.

 BakerBooks

a division of Baker Publishing Group
www.bakerbooks.com